Dr. Jaerock Lee

Keep Watching and Praying

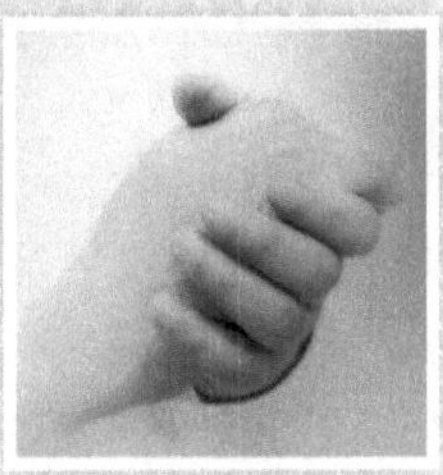

*And [Jesus] came to the disciples
and found them sleeping, and said to Peter,
"So, you men could not keep watch
with Me for one hour?
Keep watching and praying
that you may not enter into temptation;
the spirit is willing, but the flesh is weak."*
(Matthew 26:40-41)

Keep Watching and Praying by Dr. Jaerock Lee
Published by Urim Books (President: Seongnam Vin)
73, Yeouidaebang-ro 22-gil, Dongjak-gu, Seoul, Korea
www.urimbooks.com

All rights reserved. This book or parts thereof may not be reproduced in any form, stored in a retrieval system, or transmitted in any form or by any means, electronic, mechanical, photocopying, recording or otherwise, without prior written permission of the publisher.

Unless otherwise noted, all Scripture quotations are taken from the Holy Bible, NEW AMERICAN STANDARD BIBLE, ®, Copyright © 1960, 1962, 1963, 1968, 1971, 1972, 1973, 1975, 1977, 1995 by The Lockman Foundation. Used by permission.

Copyright © 2018 by Dr. Jaerock Lee
ISBN: 978-89-7557-088-9, ISBN: 978-89-7557-060-5(set)
Translation Copyright © 2007 by Dr. Esther K. Chung. Used by permission.

First Published in February 2007
Second Edition: June 2018

Previously published into Korean by Urim Books in 1992

Edited by Dr. Geumsun Vin
Designed by Design Team of Urim Books
Printed by Prione Printing
For more information contact at urimbook@hotmail.com

A Message on Publication

As God commands us to pray continually, He also instructs us in many ways on why we must pray continually and warns us to pray so that we will not fall into temptation.

Just as regular breathing is not a difficult task for a person in a state of robust good health, a spiritually healthy individual finds it natural and does not find it arduous to live by God's Word and pray continually as usual. This is because as much as one prays, he will enjoy good health and all may go well with him even as his soul gets along well. The significance of prayer, therefore, could never be stressed enough.

A person whose life has expired cannot breathe through his nostrils. By the same token, an individual whose spirit has died is unable to take spiritual breath. In other words, man's spirit was put to death because of Adam's sin, but those whose spirit has since been restored by the Holy Spirit must never fail to pray as long as their spirits are alive, just as we cannot take a break from breathing.

New believers who have only recently accepted Jesus Christ are like infants. They do not know how to pray and tend to find praying wearisome. However, when they do not give up relying on the Word of God and keeping praying diligently, their spirits will grow and become strengthened as they pray vigorously. These people will then realize they cannot live without praying, just as no one would be able to live without breathing.

Prayer is not only our spiritual breath but a channel of dialogue between God and His children, which must always remain open. The fact that conversation has been cut off between many parents and their children in modern families today is nothing short of a tragedy. Mutual trust has been destroyed and their relationships are a mere formality. However, there is nothing which we could not tell our God.

Our almighty God is a caring Father who knows and understands us the best, pays closest attention to us at all times, and desires for us to speak to Him time and again. For all believers, therefore, prayer is a key to knock and unlock the door to the heart of the almighty God and a weapon that transcends time and space. Have we not seen, heard of, and experienced firsthand countless Christians whose lives have been transformed and the direction of world history's having been altered because of powerful prayer?

As we humbly ask for the aid of the Holy Spirit when we pray, God will fill us with the Holy Spirit, allow us to more lucidly understand His will and live by it, and enable us to overcome the enemy devil and be victorious in this world. However, when one fails to receive guidance of the Holy Spirit because he does not pray, he will rely first and more on his own thought and theory, and live in untruth that is against the will of God, and it will be difficult for him to receive salvation. That is why the Bible in

Colossians 4:2 tells us, *"Devote yourselves to prayer, keeping alert in it with an attitude of thanksgiving,"* and in Matthew 26:41, *"Keep watching and praying that you may not enter into temptation; the spirit is willing, but the flesh is weak."*

The reason God's one and only Son Jesus could accomplish all His work in accordance with the will of God was because of the power of prayer. Before He began His public ministry, our Lord Jesus fasted for 40 days and set an example of a life of prayer by praying whenever He could even during His three-year ministry.

We find many Christians recognize the importance of prayer, but many of them fail to receive God's answers because they do not know how to pray according to the will of God. I have been heartbroken to see and hear of such individuals for a long time, but I am very delighted to publish a book on prayer based on over 20 years of ministry and firsthand experiences.

I hope this small book will be of great help to every reader in meeting and experiencing God, and leading a life of powerful prayer. May each reader be vigilant and pray continually so that he will enjoy good health and all may go well with him even as his soul will get along well, in the name of our Lord I pray!

Jaerock Lee

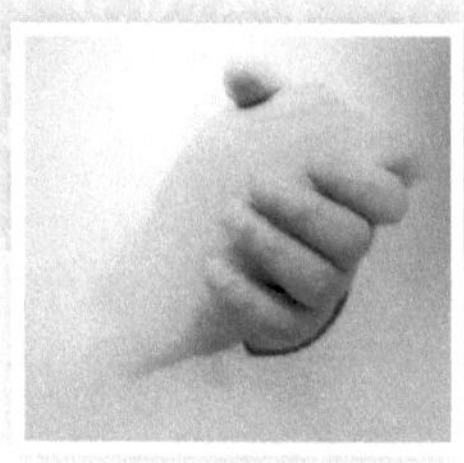

Contents

Keep Watching and Praying

A Message on Publication

Chapter 1

Ask, Seek, and Knock

"Ask, and it will be given to you;
seek,and you will find;
knock, and it will be opened to you.
For everyone who asks receives,
and he who seeks finds,
and to him who knocks it will be opened.
Or what man is there among you who,
when his son asks for a loaf, will give him a stone?
Or if he asks for a fish,
he will not give him a snake, will he?
If you then, being evil, know how to give good gifts to your
children,
how much more will your Father who is in heaven
give what is good to those who ask Him!"

Matthew 7:7-11

1. God Gives Good Gifts to Those Who Ask

God does not want His children to suffer from poverty and disease but desires every affair in their lives to go well. However, if we just sit idly without making any effort, we will not reap anything. Although God could give us everything in the universe for everything in the universe belongs to Him, He wants His children to ask, seek, and achieve on their own just as there is an old saying, "You'd feed the crying baby."

If there is a person who wishes to receive everything as he idly stands by, he is no different from flowers planted in a garden. How disheartened would parents be if their children behaved like stationary plants and spend all day in bed without making efforts to live their own lives? Such behavior is like that of a lazy man who wastes all his time waiting for a fruit from a tree to fall into his mouth.

God wants us to become His wise and assiduous children who zealously ask, seek, and knock, thereby enjoying His blessings and giving glory to Him. That is precisely why He commands us to ask, seek, and knock. No parent will give his child a stone when the child asks for bread. No parent will give her child a snake when the child asks for a fish. Even if a parent is so evil, he desires to give good gifts to his children. Don't you think our God – who loved us to the extent of giving His only begotten Son to die on our behalf – will give His children good gifts when they ask?

In John 15:16 Jesus tells us, *"You did not choose Me but I chose you, and appointed you that you would go and bear fruit, and that your fruit would remain, so that whatever you ask of the Father in My name He may give to you."* This is the solemn promise of the almighty God of love that when we zealously ask, seek, and knock, He will open the gates of heaven, bless us, and even answer the desires of our heart.

With the passage on which this Chapter is based, let us learn how to ask, seek, and knock and receive everything we ask for from God so that it will be great glory for Him and great joy for us.

2. Ask and It Will Be Given to You

God tells all people, "Ask and it will be given to you," and desires everyone to be a blessed person who receives everything for which he asks. For what, then, is He telling us to ask?

1) Ask for God's Strength and Seeing His Face

God, after He created the heavens and the earth and everything therein, created man. And He blessed and told the man to be fruitful and multiply, and fill the earth, and subdue it;

and rule over the fish of the sea and over the birds of the sky and over every living thing that moves on the earth.

After the first man Adam disobeyed God's Word, however, he lost those blessings and hid from God upon hearing His voice (Genesis 3:8). In addition, mankind who became sinners have been estranged from God and driven into the path to destruction as the slaves to the enemy devil.

For these sinners, the God of love sent His Son Jesus Christ on the earth to save them, and opened the door to their salvation. And if anyone accepts Jesus Christ as his personal Savior and believes in His name, God forgives him of all his sins and gives him the gift of the Holy Spirit.

Furthermore, the faith in Jesus Christ leads us to salvation and enables us to receive the strength of God. Only when God gives us His strength and power, can we successfully lead religious lives. In other words, only by the grace and strength from the above, can we overcome the world and live according to the Word of God. And we need to receive His power to defeat the devil.

Psalm 105:4 tells us, *"Seek the LORD and His strength; Seek His face continually."* Our God is *"I AM WHO I AM"* (Exodus 3:14), Maker of the heavens and the earth (Genesis 2:4), and Governor of all history and everything in the universe from the beginning and forever. God is the Word and by the

Word He created everything in the universe and thus, His Word is power. For man's words always change, they carry no power to create or make things happen. Unlike the words of man that are untruthful and always changing, the Word of God is alive and full of power, and can bring about the work of the creation.

Therefore, no matter how powerless one may be, if he hears the Word of God that is living and believes it without doubting, he, too, can bring about the work of the creation and create something from nothing. The creation of something from nothing is impossible without one's faith in God's Word. That is why Jesus proclaimed to all those who came before Him, *"It shall be done for you as you have believed"* (Matthew 8:13). In sum, to ask for the strength of God is the same as asking Him to give us faith.

What, then, does it mean to "seek His face continually"? Just as we cannot be said to "know" someone without knowing his face, "seeking His face" refers to the effort we are to make in discovering "who God is." It means those who have previously avoided seeing God's face and hearing His voice now open their hearts, seek and understand God, and try to hear His voice. A sinner is unable to lift up his head and tries to turn his face away from others. Once he receives forgiveness, however, he can lift his head up and see other people.

By the same token, all men have been sinners through the

disobedience to God's Word, but if one is forgiven by accepting Jesus Christ and becomes God's child by receiving the Holy Spirit, he can now see God who Himself is the Light, for he is declared to be righteous by the righteous God.

The most crucial reason God tells all people to "ask for seeing God's face" is because He wants each of them – the sinners – to be reconciled to God and receive the Holy Spirit by asking for seeing God's face, and to become His child who can come face to face with Him. When one becomes a child of God the Creator, he will receive heaven and eternal life and happiness, above which nothing else is a greater blessing.

2) Ask for Accomplishing God's kingdom and righteousness

A person who received the Holy Spirit and became a child of God is able to live a new life, for he has been reborn of the Spirit. God who deems more precious one soul over the heavens and the earth tells us His children to ask to fulfill His kingdom and righteousness above all else (Matthew 6:33).

Jesus tells us as follows in Matthew 6:25-33:

For this reason I say to you, do not be worried about your life, as to what you will eat or what you will drink; nor for your body, as to what you will put *on. Is not life more than food, and the body more than clothing? Look at the birds of the air, that they do not sow, nor reap nor gather into barns, and yet your heavenly Father feeds them. Are you not worth much more than they? And who of you by being worried can add a single hour to his life? And why are you worried about clothing? Observe how the lilies of the field grow; they do not toil nor do they spin, yet I say to you that not even Solomon in all his glory clothed himself like one of these. But if God so clothes the grass of the field, which is alive today and tomorrow is thrown into the furnace, will He not much more clothe you? You of little faith! Do not worry then, saying, `What will we eat?' or `What will we drink?' or `What will we wear for clothing?' For the Gentiles eagerly seek all these things; for your heavenly Father knows that you need all these things. But seek first His kingdom and His righteousness, and all these things will be added to you.*

What, then, is "seeking God's kingdom" and what is "seeking His righteousness"? In other words, for what shall we ask for accomplishing God's kingdom and His righteousness?

For the mankind who had been slaves to the enemy devil and destined to destruction, God sent His one and only Son to the earth and allowed Jesus to die on a cross. Through Jesus Christ,

God has also restored us the authority we lost and permitted us to walk on the path to salvation. The more we spread the news of Jesus Christ who died for us and resurrected, the more of Satan's force is destroyed. The more of Satan's force is destroyed, the more lost souls will arrive at salvation. The more lost souls arrive at salvation, the more expanded will God's kingdom be. So, "Seeking God's kingdom" refers to praying for the work of saving souls or world mission, so that all people may become God's children.

We used to live in darkness and in the midst of sin and evil, but through Jesus Christ we have been empowered to come before God who Himself is the light. For God dwells in goodness, in righteousness, and in the light, with sin and evil we could not come before Him nor become His children.

Therefore, "seeking God's righteousness" refers to praying that one's dead spirit may be revived, his soul prosper and he become righteous by living according to God's Word. We have to ask God to allow us to hear and become enlightened by God's Word, come out from sin and darkness and dwell in the light, and become sanctified by taking after God's holiness.

Casting off works of the flesh according to the desires of the Holy Spirit and becoming sanctified by living by the truth are accomplishing God's righteousness. Moreover, as we ask for accomplishing God's righteousness we will enjoy good health and all may go well with us even as our souls are prospering (3

John 1:2). That is why God commands us to ask first for accomplishing God's kingdom and His righteousness, and promises us that everything else we ask for will be given to us as well.

3) Ask to become His worker and carry out God-given duties

If you ask to fulfill God's kingdom and righteousness, you must then pray to become His worker. If you are already His worker, you must earnestly pray to carry out God-given duties. God rewards those who earnestly seek Him (Hebrews 11:6) and will render His rewards to every man according to what he has done (Revelation 22:12).

Revelation 2:10 tells us, *"Be faithful until death, and I will give you the crown of life."* Even in this life, when one studies diligently he could receive scholarships and enter a good college. When one works hard at his work, he can be promoted and receive better treatment and higher salary.

By the same token, when God's children are faithful to their God-given duties, they will be given greater duties and greater rewards. Rewards of this world are no match for rewards in the kingdom of heaven in size or glory. Therefore, at his own position each of us must become eager in faith and pray to become God's precious worker.

If one does not yet have a God-given duty, he must pray to become a worker for God's kingdom. If one has already been given a duty, he must pray to carry it out well and look to a greater duty. A layman must pray to become a deacon while the deacon must pray to become an elder. A cell leader ought to pray to become a sub-district leader, the sub-district leader to become a district leader, and the district leader to rise above that.

This is not to say one should ask for the title of an elder or a deacon. It refers to desiring to be faithful to his duties, making most efforts towards them, and serving and being used in a greater capacity by God.

The most important thing for a person who has God-given duties is the kind of faithfulness by which he is more than able to carry out even greater duties than the duties he has currently. For this, he has to pray so that God may commend him, "Well done, good and faithful servant!"

1 Corinthians 4:2 tells us, *"In this case, moreover, it is required of stewards that one be found trustworthy."* Therefore, each of us must pray to become God's faithful worker at our churches, the body of Christ, and at our different positions.

4) Ask for daily bread

In order to redeem man from his poverty, Jesus was born

poor. In order to heal every disease and infirmity, Jesus was flogged and shed His blood. Thus, it is only natural for God's children to enjoy abundant and healthy lives, and have every affair in their lives go well.

When we first ask for accomplishing God's kingdom and righteousness, He tells us that all these things will be given to us as well (Matthew 6:33). In other words, after asking for the fulfillment of God's kingdom and righteousness, we are to pray for things necessary to live in this world, such as food, clothing, shelter, work, blessings at our jobs, wellbeing of our families, and the like. God will then fill us just as He has promised. Bear in mind that if we ask for such things for our lustful desires and not for His glory, God will not answer our prayer. Prayer of sinful desires has nothing to do with God.

3. Seek and You Will Find

If you are "seeking," that means you have lost something. God wants people to possess that "something" they have lost. For He commands us to seek, we must first determine what it is that we have lost so that we can search for that "something" we have lost. We must also figure out how we are to find it.

What, then, have we lost and how do we "seek" it?

The first person God created was a living being composed of

spirit, soul, and body. As a living being who could communicate with God who is Spirit, the first man enjoyed all the blessings God had given him and lived by His Word.

Yet, after being tempted by Satan, that first man disobeyed God's command. In Genesis 2:16-17 we find, *"The LORD God commanded the man, saying, 'From any tree of the garden you may eat freely; but from the tree of the knowledge of good and evil you shall not eat, for in the day that you eat from it you will surely die.'"*

Even though the whole duty of man is to fear God and keep His commandments (Ecclesiastes 12:13), the first man created did not keep God's command. In the end, as God had warned him, after he ate from the tree of the knowledge of good and evil, his spirit in him died and he became a man of soul, no longer able to communicate with God. In addition, spirits of all his descendants died and they became men of flesh, no longer able to keep their whole duty. Adam was driven out from the Garden of Eden to the cursed ground. He and all who came after him now had to live amidst sorrow, suffering, and disease, and only by the sweat of their brow could they eat. Furthermore, they could no longer live in a manner worthy of the purpose of God's creation but as they pursued meaningless things in accordance with their thought, they became corrupt.

In order for an individual whose spirit has died and is only of his soul and flesh to live again in a manner worthy of the purpose of God's creation, he needs to recover his lost spirit. Only when the dead spirit within a man is revived, does he become a man of spirit, and communicate with God who is Spirit, and will he be able to live like a true man. This is why God commands us to seek our lost spirit.

God opened for all people a path to revive their dead spirit and that path is Jesus Christ. When we believe in Jesus Christ, as God promised us, we will receive the Holy Spirit and the Holy Spirit will come and dwell within us, and bring back to life our dead spirit. When we seek God's face and receive Jesus Christ after hearing His knocking on the door to our heart, the Holy Spirit will come and give birth to spirit (John 3:6). As we live in obedience to the Holy Spirit, cast off the works of flesh, zealously listen to, take in, make bread of, and pray on God's Word, with His aid we will be able to live by His Word. This is the process in which the dead spirit is revived and one becomes a man of spirit and recovers the lost image of God.

When we want to consume the highly nutritious yolk of an egg, we must first crack the eggshell and remove the white. In the same manner, in order for an individual to become a man of spirit, his work of flesh must be cast off and he has to give birth to spirit by the Holy Spirit. This is the "seeking" of which God spoke.

Suppose all electrical systems in the world were shut down.

No expert working alone could restore the systems. It would take a great deal of time for the expert to dispatch electricians and produce necessary parts so the electricity will be restored to every part of the world.

Likewise, in order to revive the dead spirit and become a man of complete spirit, one needs to hear and know the Word of God. Yet, for knowing the Word alone is not enough in making him a man of spirit, he must diligently take in, make bread, and pray on the Word so that he can live by God's Word.

4. Knock and the Door Will Be Opened to You

"The door" of which God spoke is a door of promise that will be opened when we knock on it. On what kind of door did God tell us to knock? It is the door to the heart of our God.

Before we knocked on the door to the heart of our God, He knocked on the doors to our heart first (Revelation 3:20). As a result, we opened the doors to our heart and accepted Jesus Christ. Now, it is our turn to knock on the door to His heart. For the heart of our God is wider than the heavens and deeper than the ocean, when we knock on the door to His immeasurable heart, we can receive anything.

As we pray and knock on the door to God's heart, He will open the gates of heaven and pour treasure upon us. When God, who opens and no one will shut, and who shuts and no one opens, opens the gates of heaven and vows to bless us, no one can stand in His way and the flood of blessing (Revelation 3:7).

We can receive God's answers when we knock on the door to His heart. Yet, depending on how much one knocks on that door, he can receive either a great or a small blessing. If he wishes to receive a great blessing, the gates of heaven must be open wide. Thus, he needs to knock on the door to God's heart all the more and diligently and please Him.

For God is pleased and delighted when we cast off evil and live by His commandments in the truth, if we live by God's Word, we can receive whatever we ask. In other words, "knocking on the door to God's heart" refers to living by God's commandments.

When we zealously knock on the door to His heart, God will never rebuke us and say, "Why are you knocking so loudly?" It is precisely the opposite. God will be all the more delighted and desire to give us what we ask. Therefore, I hope you will knock on the door to God's heart with your deeds, receive everything you ask, and thus give great glory to God.

Have you ever caught a bird with a slingshot? I remember once hearing from one of my father's friends, who commended me on my skills in making a slingshot. The slingshot is a device crafted by carefully carving a piece of wood and shooting a stone from a rubber band tied around the Y-shaped piece of wood.

If I were to liken Matthew 7:7-11 to the slingshot, "asking" refers to finding a slingshot and a stone with which to catch a bird. Then you need to equip yourself with the ability to take a good shot at the bird. What good a slingshot and a stone would do if you did not know how to take a shot? You may want to build a target, familiarize yourself with the features of the slingshot, practice on the target, and determine and understand the best ways to catch the bird. This process is equivalent to "seeking." By reading, taking in, and making bread of the Word of God, as a child of God you are now equipping yourself with qualifications to receive His answers.

If you have equipped yourself with the ability to operate the slingshot and get good shots out of it, you must now take shots and this can be compared to "knocking." Even if a slingshot and a stone are prepared, and even if you have equipped yourself with the skills to take a shot with them, if you do not take a shot you could not catch the bird. In other words, only when we live by God's Word of which we have made bread in our heart, will we receive what we ask from Him.

Asking, seeking, and knocking are not separate processes but an intertwining procedure. Now you know for what to ask, what to seek, and on what to knock. May you give great glory to God as His blessed child as you receive answers to the desires of your heart by diligently and zealously asking, seeking, and knocking, in the name of our Lord I pray!

Chapter 2

Believe that You Have Received Them

Truly I say to you, whoever says to this mountain,
'Be taken up and cast into the sea,'
and does not doubt in his heart,
but believes that what he says is going to happen,
it will be granted him.
Therefore I say to you,
all things for which you pray and ask,
believe that you have received them,
and they will be granted you.

Mark 11:23-24

1. The Great Power of Faith

One day, Jesus' disciples accompanying Him heard their Teacher say to a fruitless fig tree, *"No longer shall there ever be any fruit from you!"* (Matthew 21:19) When they saw that the tree had withered to its roots, the disciples were amazed and inquired Jesus. In reply He told them, *"Truly I say to you, if you have faith and do not doubt, you will not only do what was done to the fig tree, but even if you say to this mountain, 'Be taken up and cast into the sea,' it will happen."* (Matthew 21:21).

Jesus also promised us, *"Truly, truly, I say to you, he who believes in Me, the works that I do, he will do also; and greater works than these he will do; because I go to the Father. Whatever you ask in My name, that will I do, so that the Father may be glorified in the Son. If you ask Me anything in My name, I will do it."* (John 14:12-14), and *"If you abide in Me, and My words abide in you, ask whatever you wish, and it will be done for you. My Father is glorified by this, that you bear much fruit, and so prove to be My disciples."* (John 15:7-8).

In short, because God the Creator is the Father of those who have accepted Jesus Christ, they can have the desires of their heart answered when they believe in and obey God's Word. In Matthew 17:20 Jesus tells us, *"Because of the littleness of your faith; for truly I say to you, if you have faith the size of a mustard seed, you will say to this mountain, 'Move from here to there,' and it will move; and nothing will be impossible to you."* Why, then, do so many people fail to receive God's answers and give glory to Him despite countless hours of prayer? Let us examine how we can give glory to God as we receive everything for which we pray and ask.

2. Believe in the Almighty God

For a man to sustain his life from the moment of his birth, he would require such necessary items as food, clothing, shelter and the like. Yet, the most integral element to sustaining life is breathing; it allows life's existence possible and makes living worthwhile. While the children of God who have accepted Jesus Christ and have been reborn also require many things in life, the most fundamental of all in their lives is prayer.

Prayer is the channel of dialogue with God who is Spirit as well as breathing for our spirit. Moreover, for prayer is also a means to ask God and receive His answers, the most significant aspect in praying is the heart with which we believe in the almighty God. Depending on the degree of one's belief in God as he prays, he will feel the certainty of God's answers and will receive the answers according to his faith.

Now, who is this God in whom we place our faith?

In describing Himself in Revelation 1:8, God said *"I am the Alpha and the Omega, who is and who was and who is to come, the Almighty."* God featured in the Old Testament is the Creator of everything in the universe (Genesis 1:1-31) and divided the Red Sea and then allowed the Israelites who had left Egypt to cross it (Exodus 14:21-29). When the Israelites obeyed God's command and marched around the city of Jericho for seven days and gave a loud shout, the seemingly indestructible walls of Jericho came crumbling down (Joshua 6:1-21). When Joshua prayed to God in the middle of the battle against the Amorites, God had the sun stand still, and the moon stop (Joshua 10:12-14).

In the New Testament, Jesus, the Son of the almighty God, raised the dead from the grave (John 11:17-44), healed every disease and sickness (Matthew 4:23-24), opened the eyes of the blind (John 9:6-11), and had the crippled stand up and walk again (Acts 3:1-10). He also drove away at once the force of the enemy devil and evil spirits by His Word (Mark 5:1-20) and with five loaves of bread and two fish, He provided enough food for 5,000 men to eat and be satisfied (Mark 6:34-44). Moreover, by calming wind and waves, He showed us firsthand that He is the Governor of all things in the universe (Mark 4:35-39).

Therefore, we must believe in the almighty God who gives us

good gifts in His abundant love. Jesus told us in Matthew 7:9-11, *"Or what man is there among you who, when his son asks for a loaf, will give him a stone? Or if he asks for a fish, he will not give him a snake, will he? If you then, being evil, know how to give good gifts to your children, how much more will your Father who is in heaven give what is good to those who ask Him!"* The God of love wants to give us His children the best gifts.

In His overflowing love God gave us His one and only Son. What more would He not give us? Isaiah 53:5-6 tells us, *"But He was pierced through for our transgressions, He was crushed for our iniquities; the chastening for our well-being fell upon Him, and by His scourging we are healed. All of us like sheep have gone astray, each of us has turned to his own way; but the LORD has caused the iniquity of us all to fall on Him."* Through Jesus Christ God prepared for us, we have received life from death, and we can enjoy peace and be healed.

If God's children serve the almighty and living God as their Father and believe that God causes all things to work together for good to those who love Him and answers those crying out to Him, they must not worry or become anxious in times of temptation and affliction, but instead give thanks, rejoice, and pray.

This is to "believe in God" and He is pleased to see such display of one's faith. God also answers us according to our faith and by showing us the evidence of His existence, God allows us to give glory to Him.

3. Ask in Faith and Do Not Doubt

God the Creator of the heavens, the earth, and mankind allowed man to record the Bible so that His will and providence would be made known to all. At all times, God also shows Himself to those who believe in and obey His Word, and proves to us that He is alive and almighty through manifestations of miraculous signs and wonders.

We can believe in the living God merely by looking at the creation (Romans 1:20) and give glory to God by receiving His answers with our prayer accompanied by our faith in Him.

There are "fleshly faith" by which we can believe because our knowledge or thought is congruent with God's Word and "spiritual faith," the kind of faith by which we can receive His answers. While what the Word of God tells us is implausible when measured against man's knowledge and thought, when we ask Him by faith in Him, God gives us faith and a sense of certainty. These elements crystallize into an answer and this is spiritual faith.

Therefore, James 1:6-8 tells us, *"But he must ask in faith without any doubting, for the one who doubts is like the surf of the sea, driven and tossed by the wind. For that man ought not to expect that he will receive anything from the Lord, being a double-minded man, unstable in all his ways."*

Doubting originates from man's knowledge, thought, arguments, and pretension, and is brought to us by the enemy devil. A doubting heart is double-minded and cunning, and God detests it the most. How tragic would it be if your children could not believe but instead doubted whether you were their biological father or mother? By the same token, how could God answer the prayers of His children if they are unable to believe Him to be their Father, although He bore and nurtured them?

We are thus reminded that *"The mind set on the flesh is hostile toward God; for it does not subject itself to the law of God, for it is not even able to do so, and those who are in the flesh cannot please God"* (Romans 8:7-8), and urged to *"destroy speculations and every lofty thing raised up against the knowledge of God, and we are taking every thought captive to the obedience of Christ"* (2 Corinthians 10:5).

When our faith is transformed into spiritual faith and we do not doubt even a bit, God is thoroughly pleased and will give us anything for which we ask. When neither Moses nor Joshua doubted but only acted by faith, they could part the Red Sea, cross the Jordan River, and destroy the walls of Jericho. In the same manner, when you say to a mountain, "Be taken up and cast into the sea" and do not doubt in your heart but believe that what you say will happen, it will be done for you.

Suppose you said to Mount Everest, "Go throw yourself into the Indian Ocean." Would you receive the answer to your prayer? It is self-evident that a global chaos will follow if Mount Everest were actually thrown into the Indian Ocean. For this could not be and is not God's will, such prayer will go unanswered no matter how much you pray because He will not give you spiritual faith by which you can believe in Him.

If you are praying to accomplish something that is against God's will, the kind of faith by which you can believe in your heart will not come to you. You may believe at first your prayer may be answered but as time passes, doubts will begin to grow. Only when we pray and ask in accordance with the will of God without doubting even a little do we receive His answers. Therefore, if your prayer has not yet been answered, you must realize that it is because you have asked for something that stands against the will of God or that you are at fault for doubting or having doubted His Word.

1 John 3:21-22 reminds us, *"Beloved, if our heart does not condemn us, we have confidence before God; and whatever we ask we receive from Him, because we keep His commandments and do the things that are pleasing in His sight."*

People obeying God's commands and doing what pleases

Him do not ask for things running counter to God's will. We can receive anything we ask as long as our prayer is in accordance with His will. God tells us, *"All things for which you pray and ask, believe that you have received them, and they will be granted you"* (Mark 11:24).

Therefore, in order to receive God's answers, you must receive first from Him the spiritual faith which He gives you when you act and live by His Word. As you destroy all the arguments and speculations raised up against the knowledge of God, the doubts will disappear and you will come to possess spiritual faith, thereby receiving anything you ask.

4. All things for which you pray and ask, believe that you have received them

Numbers 23:19 reminds us, *"God is not a man, that He should lie, nor a son of man, that He should repent; has He said, and will He not do it? Or has He spoken, and will He not make it good?"*

If you truly believe in God, ask by faith, and do not doubt even a little, you must believe that you have received everything for which you asked and prayed. God is almighty and faithful, and He promises to answer us.

Why, then, do so many people say they failed to receive His

answers despite their prayer by faith? Is this because God did not answer them? No. God has surely answered their prayer but it is taking time because they have not prepared themselves as vessels worthy of containing His answers.

When a farmer sows seeds, he believes he will reap fruit but cannot gather the fruit immediately. After seeds have been sown, they bud, flower, and bear fruit. Some seeds take longer in bearing fruit than others. Likewise, the process of receiving God's answers requires such sowing and nurturing procedures.

Suppose some student prayed, "Allow me to enter and study at Harvard University." If he prayed by the faith in His power, God will surely answer the student's prayer. However, the answer to his prayer may not come to him right away. God prepares the student to grow to be a vessel proper for His answers and at a later time He will answer the prayer. God will give him the heart to study hard and diligently so that he may excel at school. As the student keeps on praying, God will remove from his mind any worldly thoughts and give him wisdom and enlighten him to study more effectively. According to the student's deeds, God will manage every affair in his life to go favorably and equip the student with qualifications to enter Harvard and when the time arrives, God will allow him to enter Harvard.

The same rule applies to people stricken by disease. As they learn through God's Word why diseases come about and how they can be healed, when they pray by faith they can receive healing. They must discover the wall of sin that stands between themselves and God and get to the bottom of the source of the disease. If the disease came about because of hatred, they must cast off hatred and transform their heart to that of love. If the disease was brought forth by overeating, they must receive from God the power to self-control and fix their harmful habit. Only through such processes does God give people faith by which they can believe and prepare them to be proper vessels to receive His answers.

Praying for prosperity at one's business is no different from cases above. If you pray to receive blessings through your business, God will first put you to the test to become a vessel worthy of His blessing. He will give you wisdom and power so that your ability to run the business becomes distinguished, so that your business will grow larger, and so that you will be led to an excellent situation in which to run the business. He will lead you to trustworthy individuals, gradually increase your income, and cultivate your business. When the time of His choosing comes, He will respond just as you prayed.

Through these sowing and nurturing processes, God will lead your soul to prosper and put you to the test to make you into a vessel worthy of receiving whatever you ask Him. Therefore, you must never grow impatient based on your own thought. Instead, you ought to adjust yourselves on God's timeframe and wait for His time, believing that you have already received His answers.

The almighty God, according to the laws of the spiritual realm, answers His children in His justice and is pleased when they ask Him by faith. Hebrews 11:6 reminds us, *"And without faith it is impossible to please Him, for he who comes to God must believe that He is and that He is a rewarder of those who seek Him."*

May you please God by possessing the kind of faith by which you believe you have already received everything you asked for in prayer and give great glory to Him by receiving everything for which you ask, in the name of our Lord I pray!

Chapter 3

The Kind of Prayer
with which God is Pleased

And [Jesus] came out and proceeded
as was His custom to the Mount of Olives;
and the disciples also followed Him.
When He arrived at the place,
He said to them,
"Pray that you may not enter into temptation."

And He withdrew from them about a stone's throw,
and He knelt down and began to pray, saying,
"Father, if You are willing, remove this cup from Me;
yet not My will, but Yours be done."
Now an angel from heaven appeared to Him,
strengthening Him.
And being in agony He was praying very fervently;
and His sweat became like drops of blood,
falling down upon the ground.

Luke 22:39-44

1. Jesus Set an Example of Proper Prayer

Luke 22:39-44 portrays a scene in which Jesus prayed at Gethsemane the night before He was to carry the cross to open the path to salvation for all mankind. These verses tell us many aspects on the kind of attitude and heart we ought to have when praying.

How did Jesus pray so that He not only carried the heavy cross but also overcame the enemy devil? What kind of heart did Jesus take when He prayed so that God was pleased with His prayer and dispatched an angel from heaven to strengthen Him?

Based on these verses, let us delve into the proper attitude in praying and the kind of prayer with which God is pleased, and I urge each of you to examine your own life of prayer.

1) Jesus prayed habitually

God told us to pray without ceasing (1 Thessalonians 5:17) and promised us to give us when we ask to Him (Matthew 7:7). Although it is right to pray continually and ask all the time, most people pray only when they want something or have problems.

Yet, Jesus came out and proceeded as was His custom to the Mount of Olives (Luke 22:39). Prophet Daniel continued kneeling on his knees three times a day, praying and giving thanks before his God, as he had been doing previously (Daniel

6:10), and two of Jesus' disciples Peter and John set apart a certain time of the day to pray (Acts 3:1).

We must follow Jesus' example and develop a habit of setting apart a specific time and praying continually everyday. God is especially pleased with people's dawn prayer by which they commit everything to God at the beginning of each day and nighttime prayer by which they give thanks for God's protection during the day at the end of each day. Through these prayers you can receive His great power.

2) Jesus knelt down to pray

When you kneel, the heart with which you pray stands upright and you show reverence to the people to whom you speak. It is only natural for anyone who prays to God to kneel down when he prays.

Jesus the Son of God prayed with a humble attitude as He knelt down to pray to the almighty God. King Solomon (1 Kings 8:54), the apostle Paul (Acts 20:36), and Deacon Stephen who died a martyr (Acts 7:60) all knelt down when they prayed.

When we ask our parents or someone with authority for a favor or things that we desire, we become nervous and take every precaution to prevent ourselves from making mistakes. How, then, should we appear slovenly in mind and body if we know that we are speaking to God the Creator? Kneeling down is an expression of your heart that reveres God and trusts in His power. We must tidy up ourselves and humbly kneel down when we pray.

3) Jesus' prayer was in accordance with the will of God

Jesus prayed to God, *"Yet not My will, but Yours be done"* (Luke 22:42). Jesus the Son of God came to the earth to die on a wooden cross even though He was faultless and blameless. That is why He prayed, *"Father, if You are willing, remove this cup from Me"* (Luke 22:42). But He knew the will of God that was to save all mankind through one individual, and prayed not for His own good but only in accordance with God's will.

1 Corinthians 10:31 tells us, *"Whether, then, you eat or drink or whatever you do, do all to the glory of God."* If we ask for something that is not for the glory of God but rather the lustful desires, we are not making proper requests; we must only pray in accordance with God's will. Moreover, God tells us to keep in mind what we find in James 4:2-3, *"You lust and do not have; so you commit murder. You are envious and cannot obtain; so you fight and quarrel. You do not have because you do not ask. You ask and do not receive, because you ask with wrong motives, so that you may spend it on your pleasures."* So, we need to look back and see whether we are praying only for our own good.

4) Jesus wrestled in prayer

In Luke 22:44, we can find how sincerely Jesus prayed. *"And being in agony He was praying very fervently; and His sweat became like drops of blood, falling down upon the ground."* The climate at Gethsemane where Jesus prayed would cool down at nighttime so that it would have been difficult even to sweat. Now, can you imagine how much Jesus strained Himself in sincere and earnest prayer that His sweat became like drops of blood falling upon the ground? If Jesus had prayed in silence, could He have prayed so earnestly to sweat while praying? As Jesus cried out to God passionately and earnestly, His sweat became "like drops of blood falling to the ground."

In Genesis 3:17 God tells Adam, *"Because you have listened to the voice of your wife, and have eaten from the tree about which I commanded you, saying, 'You shall not eat from it'; Cursed is the ground because of you; In toil you will eat of it all the days of your life."* Before man was cursed, he lived a life of abundance with everything God had provided for him. When sin entered him through his disobedience to God, his communication with his Creator came to an end, and only through painful toil could he now eat.

If what is possible for us can be achieved only through painful toil, what are we to do when we ask God for something we cannot do? Please remember that only with crying out to

God in prayer, painful toil, and sweat can we receive what we desire from God. Moreover, keep in mind how God told us painful toil and effort were necessary to bear fruit and how Jesus Himself earnestly toiled and wrestled in prayer. Keep these in mind, do exactly what Jesus did, and pray in a way that is pleasing to God.

We have thus far examined how Jesus, who set an example of proper prayer, prayed. If Jesus, who possessed all authority, prayed to an extent of setting an example, with what kind of attitude should we, God's mere creatures, pray? The outward appearance and attitude of one's prayer express his heart. Therefore, the kind of heart with which we pray may be equally important as the attitude with which we pray.

2. Essentials to the Kind of Prayer with which God is Pleased

With what kind of heart should we pray so that it is pleasing to God and He will answer our prayer?

1) You must pray with all your heart

We have learned through the way Jesus prayed that prayer from one's heart stems from the attitude with which he prays to God. We can tell from the attitude, with what kind of heart one prays.

Take a look at Jacob's prayer in Genesis 32. With the Jabbok River ahead, Jacob found himself in a predicament. Jacob could not go back because he had made a deal with his uncle Laban that he would not cross a boundary line called Galeed. He could not cross the Jabbok where, on the other side, his brother Esau was waiting with 400 men to capture Jacob. It was at such a desperate time when Jacob's pride and ego on which he had been relying was utterly destroyed. Jacob finally realized that only when he committed his everything to God and moved His heart could his problems be solved. As Jacob wrestled in prayer to the point of having his hip joint broken, he finally received God's answer. Jacob was able to move God's heart and reconcile with his brother who had been waiting to deal with him.

Take a close look at 1 Kings 18 in which Prophet Elijah received God's "fiery answer" and gave great glory to God. When idolatry was thriving during King Ahab's reign, Elijah single-handedly contended with 450 prophets of Baal and defeated them by bringing down God's answers before the Israelites and bore witness to the living God.

This was the time when Ahab thought Prophet Elijah was to blame for the three-and-a-half-year drought inflicted upon Israel and was looking for the prophet. However, when God ordered Elijah to go before Ahab, the prophet quickly obeyed. As the prophet went before the king who had been looking to kill him, boldly spoke what God was speaking through him, and reversed everything with prayer of faith that contained not one bit of doubt, a work of repentance was manifested for people who had been worshipping idols as they returned to God. Moreover, Elijah crouched down on the earth and put his face between his knees when he earnestly prayed that he would bring down God's work on the earth and put an end to the drought that had tormented the land for three and a half years (1 Kings 18:42).

Our God reminds us in Ezekiel 36:36-37, *"'I, the LORD, have spoken and will do it.' Thus says the LORD GOD, 'This also I will let the house of Israel ask Me to do for them.'"* In other words, even though God had promised Elijah a heavy rain on Israel, the heavy rain could not have fallen without Elijah's earnest prayer from his heart. Prayer from our heart can truly move and impress God, who will promptly answer us and allow us to give glory to Him.

2) You must cry out to God in prayer

God promises us He would listen to us and meet us when we call upon Him and come and pray to Him and seek Him with all our heart (Jeremiah 29:12-13; Proverbs 8:17). In Jeremiah 33:3 He also promises us, *"Call to Me and I will answer you, and I will tell you great and mighty things, which you do not know."* The reason God tells us to cry out to Him in prayer is because when we cry out to Him in prayer in loud voice, we will be able to pray with all our heart. In other words, when we cry out in prayer, we will be severed from worldly thoughts, fatigue, and drowsiness and our own thoughts will find no place in our mind.

Yet, many churches today believe and teach their congregations that being quiet inside the sanctuaries is "godly" and "holy." When some brethren cry out to God in a loud voice, the rest of the congregation are quick to think they are improper and even condemn such people to be heretic. This, however, has been caused without knowing God's Word and His will.

Early churches, which witnessed great manifestations of God's power and revival, could please God in the fullness of the Holy Spirit as they lifted their voices to God with one accord (Acts 4:24). Even today, we can see how countless miraculous signs and wonders are displayed and how they experience great revival at churches that cry out to God in a loud voice and follow and live by God's will.

"Crying out to God" refers to praying to God with an earnest prayer and in a raised voice. Through such prayer, brothers and sisters in Christ can become full of the Holy Spirit and, as the interfering forces of the enemy devil are driven away, they can receive answers to their prayer and spiritual gifts.

In the Bible are countless records of instances in which Jesus and many forefathers of faith cried out to God in a raised voice and received His answers.

Let us examine a few examples in the Old Testament.

In Exodus 15:22-25 is a scene in which the Israelites, after leaving Egypt much earlier, have just safely crossed the Red Sea on foot after Moses' faith parted it. For Israelites' faith was small, however, they grumbled against Moses when they could not find anything to drink as they crossed the Desert of Shur. When Moses "cried out" to God, the bitter water of Marah turned sweet.

In Numbers 12 is a scene in which Moses' sister Miriam became leprous after she talked against him. When Moses cried out to God, saying, *"O God, heal her, I pray!"* God healed Miriam of her leprosy.

In 1 Samuel 7:9 we read, *"Samuel took a suckling lamb and offered it for a whole burnt offering to the LORD; and Samuel cried to the LORD for Israel and the LORD answered him."*

1 Kings 17 is a story of a Zarephath widow who showed Elijah the servant of God hospitality. When her son became ill and died, Elijah called to God and said, *"O LORD my God, I pray You, let this child's life return to him."* God heard the voice of Elijah, and the life of the child returned to him and he revived (1 Kings 17:21-22). When God heard Elijah's cry, we find that God answered the prophet's prayer.

Jonah, who had been swallowed by and confined inside a

great fish because of his disobedience to God, also received salvation as he cried out to God in prayer. In Jonah 2:2 we find that when he prayed, *"I called out of my distress to the LORD, And He answered me. I cried for help from the depth of Sheol; You heard my voice."* God heard his cry and saved him. No matter how a situation in which we find ourselves may be as dire and distressing as that of Jonah, God will give us the desires of our heart, answer us, and give us solutions to problems when we repent of our wrongdoings in His eyes and cry out to Him.

The New Testament is also filled with scenes in which people cried out to God.

In John 11:43-44, we find that Jesus cried out with a loud voice, *"Lazarus, come forth,"* and the man who had died came forth, bound hand and foot with wrappings, and his face was wrapped around with a cloth. It would have been no difference to the dead Lazarus whether Jesus called out in a loud voice or whispered to him. Yet, Jesus was calling out to God in a loud voice. Jesus brought Lazarus, whose body had been in the tomb for 4 days, back to life by His prayer according to God's will and displayed God's glory.

Mark 10:46-52 tells us the healing of a blind beggar named Bartimaeus:

"And as [Jesus] was leaving Jericho with His

disciples and a large crowd, a blind beggar named Bartimaeus, the son of Timaeus, was sitting by the road. When he heard that it was Jesus the Nazarene, he began to cry out and say, "Jesus, Son of David, have mercy on me!" Many were sternly telling him to be quiet, but he kept crying out all the more, "Son of David, have mercy on me!" And Jesus stopped and said, "Call him here." So they called the blind man, saying to him, "Take courage, stand up! He is calling for you." Throwing aside his cloak, he jumped up and came to Jesus. And answering him, Jesus said, "What do you want Me to do for you?" And the blind man said to Him, "Rabboni, I want to regain my sight!" And Jesus said to him, "Go; your faith has made you well." Immediately he regained his sight and began following Him on the road."

In Acts 7:59-60, as Deacon Stephen was being stoned to die a martyr, he called on the Lord and said, *"Lord Jesus, receive my spirit!"* Then falling on his knees, he cried out with a loud voice, *"Lord, do not hold this sin against them!"*

And it is read in Acts 4:23-24, 31, *"When they [Peter and John] had been released, they went to their own companions and reported all that the chief priests and the elders had said to them. And when they heard this, they lifted their voices to God with one accord. And when they had prayed, the place where they had gathered together was shaken, and they were all filled with the Holy Spirit and began to speak the word of God with boldness."*

When you cry out to God, you can become a true witness of Jesus Christ and manifest the power of the Holy Spirit.

God told us to cry out to Him even when we are fasting. If we spend much of our fasting time sleeping from fatigue, we will receive no answers from God. God promises in Isaiah 58:9, *"Then you will call, and the LORD will answer; You will cry, and He will say, 'Here I am.'"* According to His promise, if we cry out when we fast, grace and power from above will descend upon us and we will be victorious and receive God's answers.

With "The Parable of the Persistent Widow," Jesus asked us rhetorically, *"Now, will not God bring about justice for His elect who cry to Him day and night, and will He delay long over them?"* and told us to cry out in prayer (Luke 18:7).

Therefore, as Jesus tells us in Matthew 5:18, *"For truly I say to you, until heaven and earth pass away, not the smallest letter or stroke shall pass from the Law until all is accomplished,"* when God's children pray, it is only natural for them to cry out in prayer. This is God's command. For His law dictates that we are to eat the fruit of our toil, we can receive God's answers when we call out to Him.

Some people may retort, basing their claims on Matthew 6:6-

8, and ask, "Do we have to cry out to God when He already knows what we need before we even ask?" or "Why cry out when Jesus said to pray in secret in my room with the door closed?" Yet, nowhere in the Bible will you find passages referring to people's praying in secret in the comfort of their rooms.

The true meaning of Matthew 6:6-8 is urging us to pray with all our heart. Enter your inner room and close the door behind you. If you were in a room that was private and quiet with the door closed, will you not be cut off from all outside contacts? Just as we will be cut off from all outside access in our own rooms with the door closed, Jesus in Matthew 6:6-8 is telling us to cut ourselves off all of our thoughts, worldly thoughts, worries, anxieties, and the like, and pray with all our heart.

Furthermore, Jesus told this story as a lesson for people to know that God does not listen to the prayer of the Pharisees and priests, who during Jesus' time prayed in a loud voice to be commended and seen by others. We ought not to become proud of the quantity of our prayer. Instead, we must wrestle in our prayer with all our heart to Him who searches our hearts and minds, to the Almighty who knows all our needs and wants, and the One who is our "all in all."

It is difficult to pray with all our heart through silent prayer. Try praying by meditation with your eyes closed at nighttime. You will soon discover yourself struggling against fatigue and worldly thoughts, instead of praying. When you grow weary from fending off sleep, you will fall asleep before you know it.

Instead of praying in the stillness of a quiet room, *"He [Jesus] went off to the mountain to pray, and He spent the whole night in prayer to God"* (Luke 6:12) and *"In the early morning, while it was still dark, Jesus got up, left the house, and went away to a secluded place, and was praying there"* (Mark 1:35). In his roof chamber, Prophet Daniel had windows open toward Jerusalem, and he continued kneeling on his knees three times a day, praying and giving thanks before his God (Daniel 6:10). Peter went up on the roof to pray (Acts 10:9), and the apostle Paul went outside the gate to a riverside, where he was supposing that there would be a place of prayer and prayed at the place of prayer while he was staying in Philippi (Acts 16:13; 16). These people designated specific places to pray because they wanted to pray with all their heart. You must pray in a way that your prayer can penetrate the forces of the enemy devil the ruler of the kingdom of the air and be delivered to the throne above. Only then will you be filled with the Holy Spirit, have your temptations be driven away, and receive answers to all your problems big and small.

3) Your prayer must have a purpose

Some people may plant trees for good timber. Others may plant trees for fruit. Still others may plant trees to use the wood in creating a beautiful garden. If one planted trees with no particular purpose, before saplings grow tall and old he may neglect his trees because he can become preoccupied with his other work.

Having a clear purpose in any endeavor propels that endeavor and brings quicker and better results and achievements. Without a clear purpose, however, an endeavor may not be able to withstand even a small obstacle because without any direction, there are only doubts and resignation.

We must have a clear purpose when we pray before God. We have been promised to receive from God anything we ask when we are confident before Him (1 John 3:21-22), and when the purpose of our prayer is clear, we would be able to pray more earnestly with greater perseverance. Our God will, when He sees there is nothing to be condemned in our hearts, provide for us everything we need. We must always keep in mind the purpose of our prayer and be able to pray in a way that is pleasing to God.

4) You must pray by faith

For the measure of faith varies for each person, every person will receive God's answers according to his or her faith. When people first accept Jesus Christ and open up their hearts, the Holy Spirit comes to dwell in them and God seals them as His children. This is when they possess faith the size of a mustard seed.

As they keep the Lord's Day holy and keep praying, strive to keep God's commandments, and live by His Word, their faith will grow. However, when they face temptations and suffering before they stand firmly on the rock of faith, they may question God's power and become discouraged at times. However, once they stand on the rock of faith, they will not fall in any circumstances but look to God in faith and keep on praying. God sees such faith, and He will work for the good of those who love Him.

As they build up prayer upon prayer, with the power from above they will fight against sin and resemble our Lord. They will have a clear idea of our Lord's will and obey it. This is faith that is pleasing to God and they will receive anything they ask. As people arrive at this measure of faith, they will experience the promise found in Mark 16:17-18, saying, *"These signs will accompany those who have believed: in My name they will cast out demons, they will speak with new tongues; they will pick up serpents, and if they drink any deadly poison, it will not hurt them; they will lay hands on the sick, and they will recover."* People of great faith will receive answers according to their faith, and people with small faith will also receive answers according to their faith.

There are "self-centered faith" which you come to possess on your own, and "God-given faith." "Self-centered faith" is not in agreement with one's deed, but God-given faith is spiritual faith that is always accompanied by deed. The Bible tells us that faith is the assurance of things hoped for (Hebrews 11:1), but "self-centered faith" does not become a certainty. Even if one may possess faith to part the Red Sea and move a mountain, with the "self-centered faith," he does not have a certainty for God's answers.

God gives us "living faith" that is accompanied with deeds when we, according to our own faith in Him, obey, display our faith by deed, and pray. When we show Him the faith we already possess, that faith will combine with the "living faith" which He adds onto us, which in turn will become great faith by which we can receive God's answers without delay. At times people experience undeniable certainty of His answer. This is faith given to them by God and if people possess such faith, they have already received their answers.

Therefore, without doubting even a little, we must place our trust in the promise Jesus gives us in Mark 11:24, *"Therefore I say to you, all things for which you pray and ask, believe that you have received them, and they will be granted you."* And we must pray until we become certain of God's answers, and receive whatever we ask for in prayer (Matthew 21:22).

5) You must pray in love

Hebrews 11:6 tells us, *"And without faith it is impossible to please Him, for he who comes to God must believe that He is and that He is a rewarder of those who seek Him."* If we believe that all our prayers will be answered and are stored as our heavenly rewards, we would not find praying wearisome or difficult.

Just as Jesus wrestled in prayer to give life to mankind, if we pray with the love for other souls, we can pray earnestly, too. If you can pray with sincere love for others, that means you are able to put yourself in their shoes and see their problems as your own, thereby praying earnestly all the more.

For instance, suppose you pray for the construction of your church's sanctuary. You must pray with the same heart with which you would pray for the construction of your own house. Just as you would ask in detail for the land, workers, materials, and the like for your own home, you must ask for every element and factor necessary for the construction of the sanctuary in detail. If you are praying for a patient, you must put yourself in his shoes and wrestle in prayer with all your heart as if his pain and suffering were your very own.

In order to achieve God's will, Jesus habitually knelt down and wrestled in prayer in His love for God and His love for all mankind. As a result, the path to salvation opened and anyone who accepts Jesus Christ can now be forgiven of his sins and enjoy the authority to which he is entitled as a child of God.

Based on the way Jesus prayed and essentials to the kind of prayer with which God is pleased, we must examine our attitude and heart, pray with an attitude and a heart that are pleasing to God, and receive from Him everything we ask for in prayer.

Chapter 4

That You May Not Enter into Temptation

And [Jesus] came to the disciples
and found them sleeping,
and said to Peter,
"So, you men could not keep
watch with Me for one hour?
Keep watching and praying
that you may not enter into temptation;
the spirit is willing, but the flesh is weak."

Matthew 26:40-41

1. Prayer Life: Our Spirit's Breath

Our God is alive, oversees man's life, death, curse, and blessing, and of love, justice, and goodness. He does not want His children to fall into temptation or face sufferings but lead lives filled with blessings. That is why He has sent to the earth the Holy Spirit the Counselor who would help His children overcome this world, drive away the enemy devil, lead healthy and joyous lives, and arrive at salvation.

God promised us in Jeremiah 29:11-12, *"For I know the plans that I have for you, plans for welfare and not for calamity to give you a future and a hope. Then you will call upon Me and come and pray to Me, and I will listen to you."*

If we are to live this life in peace and hope, we must pray. If we pray continually during our lives in Christ, we will not be tempted, our soul will prosper, what is seemingly "impossible" will turn into "possible," every affair in life will go well, and we will enjoy good health. Yet, if God's children do not pray, for our enemy the devil prowls around like a roaring lion looking for someone to devour, we will face temptations and meet with disasters.

Just as life expires if we do not breathe everyday, the importance of prayer in the lives of God's children cannot be stressed enough. That is why God commands us to pray without ceasing (1 Thessalonians 5:17), reminds us failing to pray is a sin

(1 Samuel 12:23), and teaches us to pray that we may not enter into temptation (Matthew 26:41).

New believers who have recently accepted Jesus Christ for the first time tend to find praying difficult because they do not know how to pray. Our dead spirit is reborn when we accept Jesus Christ and receive the Holy Spirit. The spiritual condition at this time is that of an infant; it is difficult to pray.

However, if they do not give up but keep praying and making bread of God's Word, their spirits become strengthened and their prayer becomes more potent. Just as people cannot live without breathing, they come to realize they cannot live without praying.

In my childhood, there were children who competed against one another to see who could hold their breath the longest. Two children at a time would face each other and take deep breaths. When another child says "Ready~" the two children breathe in as much as they can. When the "referee" yells "Begin!" with facial expressions filled with resolve, the two children hold their breath.

At first, holding breath is not too difficult. As time passes a little, however, the children feel choked as their faces turn scorching red. In the end, they are unable to hold their breath any longer and are forced to breathe out. No one can live if his breathing stops.

It is the same with prayer. When a spiritual person stops

praying, he does not notice much of a difference at first. With the passing of time, however, his heart begins to feel disheartened and afflicted. If we could see his spirit with our eyes, that spirit may be close to being suffocated. If he realizes that all this is because he stopped praying and resumes praying, he can lead a normal life in Christ again. Yet, if he were to continue committing the sin of failing to pray, his heart will feel all the more wretched and distressed, and he will endure many aspects of his life going awry.

"Taking a break" from praying is not the will of God. Just as we gasp until our breathing returns to normal, returning to the normal prayer life of the past is more difficult and takes that much more time. The longer the "break" has been, the longer it takes to recuperate your prayer life.

People who realize that prayer is the breath of their spirits do not find praying arduous. If they have been praying habitually the way they breathe in and breathe out habitually, instead of finding praying strenuous or difficult they become more peaceful, more filled with hope, and more joyous in life than not praying. This is because they receive God's answers and give glory to Him as much as they pray.

2. Reasons Temptation Comes Across People Who Do Not Pray

Jesus set for us an example of prayer and told His disciples to watch and pray so that they would not fall into temptation (Matthew 26:41). Conversely, this means that if we do not pray continually, we are to fall into temptation. Why, then, does temptation come across people who do not pray?

God created the first man Adam, made him a living being, and allowed him to communicate with God who is Spirit. After Adam ate from the tree of the knowledge of good and evil and disobeyed God, Adam's spirit died, his communication with God was severed, and he was driven out from the Garden of Eden. As the enemy devil, the ruler of the kingdom of the air, seized control of man who could no longer communicate with God who is Spirit, man became gradually and all the more drenched in sin.

For the wages of sin is death (Romans 6:23), God unveiled His providence of salvation through Jesus Christ for all mankind who had been destined to death. God seals as His child anyone who accepts Jesus as his Savior, confesses he is a sinner, and repents, and as a token of assurance God gives him the Holy Spirit.

The Holy Spirit the Counselor whom God sent convicts the world of guilt in regard to sin and righteousness and judgment

(John 16:8), intercedes for us with groans that words cannot express (Romans 8:26), and enables us to overcome the world.

In order to be filled with the Holy Spirit and receive His guidance, prayer is absolutely necessary. Only when we pray will the Holy Spirit speak to us, move our hearts and minds, warn us of impending temptations, tell us of ways to avoid such temptations, and help us overcome temptations even if they come our way.

However, without praying there is no way to distinguish the will of God from the will of man. In pursuit of worldly desires, people without a routine prayer life will live according to their habits of old and pursue what is right according to their self-righteousness. Thus, temptations and sufferings are inflicted as they face all kinds of difficulties.

James 1:13-15 tells us, *"Let no one say when he is tempted, 'I am being tempted by God'; for God cannot be tempted by evil, and He Himself does not tempt anyone. But each one is tempted when he is carried away and enticed by his own lust. Then when lust has conceived, it gives birth to sin; and when sin is accomplished, it brings forth death."*

In other words, temptations come across people who do not pray because they fail to distinguish the will of God from the will of man, become enticed by their worldly desires, and suffer from hardships because they are unable to overcome temptations. God wants all His children to learn to be content with whatever the circumstances are, come to know what it is to be in need and what it is to have plenty, and learn the secret of being content in any and every situation, whether well fed or hungry, whether living in plenty or in want (Philippians 4:11-12).

However, for the worldly desires conceive and give birth to sin and the wages of sin is death, God cannot protect people who continue to sin. As much as people have sinned, the enemy devil brings them times of temptation and suffering. Some people who have fallen into temptations disappoint God by claiming that He dropped them into temptations and thrust them into suffering. However, these are acts of bearing a grudge against God and such individuals cannot overcome temptations and do not leave any room for God to work for their good.

Thus, God commands us to destroy speculations and every lofty thing raised up against the knowledge of God and to take every thought captive to the obedience of Christ (2 Corinthians 10:5). And He reminds us in Romans 8:6-7, *"For the mind set on the flesh is death, but the mind set on the Spirit is life and peace, because the mind set on the flesh is hostile toward God; for it does not subject itself to the law of God, for it is not even able to do so."*

Most of the information we have learned and stored in our minds as "right" before we meet God is found to be false in light of the truth. So, we can wholly follow the will of God when we destroy all theories and fleshly thoughts. Moreover, if we want to destroy arguments and every pretension and obey the truth, we must pray.

At times, the God of love corrects His beloved children so that they do not go down the path to destruction and allows them temptations so that they can repent and turn from their ways. When people examine themselves and repent of anything within them that is improper in God's sight, keep praying, look to the One who in all things works for the good of those who love Him, and rejoice always, God will see their faith and surely answer them.

3. The Spirit is Willing but the Flesh is Weak

The night before He took upon the cross, Jesus went with His disciples to a place called Gethsemane and wrestled in prayer. When He found His disciples sleeping, Jesus lamented and said, *"The spirit is willing, but the flesh is weak"* (Matthew 26:41).

In the Bible are such terms as, "flesh," "the things of the flesh," and "deeds of the flesh." On the one hand, "flesh" is contrary to "spirit" and generally refers to everything that is corrupt and changes. It refers to every creation, including man before having been transformed by the truth, plants, all animals, and the like. On the other hand, "spirit" refers to things that are everlasting, truthful, and unchanging.

Since Adam's disobedience, all men and women are born with an inherent sinful nature, and this is the original sin. "Self-committed sins" are untruthful acts committed at the instigation of the enemy devil. Man become "flesh" when untruth has smeared his body and the body is combined with the sinful nature. This is what Romans 9:8 mentions "children of the flesh." The Verse says, *"That is, it is not the children of the flesh who are children of God, but the children of the promise are regarded as descendant."* And Romans 13:14 warns us, *"Put on the Lord Jesus Christ, and make no provision for the flesh in regard to its lusts."*

Moreover, "the things of the flesh" are assortments of such various sinful attributes as deception, envy, jealousy, and hatred (Romans 8:5-8). They have not yet been acted out physically but may be induced into action. When these desires are put in motion, they are referred to as *"the deeds of the flesh"* (Galatians 5:19-21).

What did Jesus mean by "the flesh is weak"? Was he referring to the physical condition of His disciples? As former fishermen, Peter, James, and John were men at the pinnacle of life and of robust good health. For people who had spent many nights fishing, staying awake for a few hours at night should not have been a big deal. However, even after Jesus told them to stay there and keep watch with Him, the three disciples were unable to pray but ended up falling asleep. They may have gone to Gethsemane to pray with Jesus, but this desire was only in their heart. Instead, when Jesus told them their flesh was "weak," He meant the three of them were unable to thwart the lust of the flesh that enticed them to sleep and rest.

Peter who was one of Jesus' beloved disciples could not pray because his flesh was weak even though his spirit was willing, and when Jesus was captured and his life was threatened, three times he denied having known Jesus. This took place prior to Jesus' resurrection and ascension into heaven, and Peter was trapped in deep fear without having received the Holy Spirit. After Peter received the Holy Spirit, however, he brought the dead back to life, manifested miraculous signs and wonders, and grew bold enough to be crucified upside down. Signs of Peter's weakness were nowhere to be found as he was transformed into a bold apostle of God's power who was not afraid of death. This is because Jesus shed His precious, spotless, and blameless blood and redeemed us from our infirmities, poverty, and weakness. If we live by faith, in obedience to the Word of God, we will enjoy good health in both body and spirit, and be able to do what is impossible for man, and anything will be possible for us.

At times, some people who commit sins, however, instead of repenting of their sins, are quick to say "The flesh is weak" and think it is natural to sin. Such people utter such words because they are not aware of the truth. Suppose a father gave his son $1,000. How ridiculous would it be if the son put the money in his pocket and said to his father, "I don't have any money; not even a dime"? How frustrating would it be for the father if his son—still with the $1,000 in his pocket—starves himself without purchasing any food? Therefore, for those of us who have received the Holy Spirit, "The flesh is weak" is an oxymoron.

I have seen many people who used to go to bed at 10 o'clock at night, now attending "The Friday All-night Service" after praying and receiving the Holy Spirit's help. They do not grow tired or drowsy and give every Friday night to God in the fullness of the Holy Spirit. This is because, in the fullness of the Holy Spirit, people's spiritual eyes have become sharpened, their hearts are overflowing with joy, they do not feel fatigue, and their bodies feel lighter.

For we are living in the era of the Holy Spirit, we must never fail to pray or commit a sin because "the flesh is weak." Instead, by keeping ourselves alert and praying continually, we must receive the aid of the Holy Spirit and cast off the things and the deeds of the flesh and the like, and zealously lead our lives in Christ by always living according to God's will for us.

4. Blessings for People Keeping Themselves Alert and Praying

1 Peters 5:8-9 tells us, *"Be of sober spirit, be on the alert. Your adversary, the devil, prowls around like a roaring lion, seeking someone to devour. But resist him, firm in your faith, knowing that the same experiences of suffering are being accomplished by your brethren who are in the world."* The enemy Satan and the devil, the ruler of the kingdom of the air, strive to entice believers in God to go astray and prevent His people from possessing faith every chance they get.

If someone wants to uproot a tree, he would first try shaking it. If the trunk is big and thick and the tree is rooted too deep in the ground, he will give up and try shaking another tree. When it seems that the second tree can be uprooted more easily than the first, he will become all the more determined and shake the tree even harder. By the same token, the enemy devil that seeks to entice us will be driven away if we remain firm. If we are shaken even a bit, however, the enemy devil will keep on bringing us temptations to knock us down.

In order to discern and destroy the enemy devil's schemes and walk in the light by living according to God's Word, we must wrestle in prayer and receive God-given strength and power from above. Jesus the one and only Son of God could accomplish everything according to the will of God because of the power of prayer. Before He began His public ministry, Jesus prepared Himself by fasting forty days and forty nights, and throughout His three-year ministry He manifested amazing works of God's power by praying habitually and continually. At the end of His public ministry, Jesus could destroy the authority of death and overcome through resurrection because He wrestled in prayer at Gethsemane. That is why our Lord urged us to *"Devote yourselves to prayer, keeping alert in it with an attitude of thanksgiving"* (Colossians 4:2), and *"The end of all things is near; therefore, be of sound judgment and sober spirit for the purpose of prayer"* (1 Peter 4:7). He also taught us to pray, *"And do not lead us into temptation, but deliver us from evil"* (Matthew 6:13). Preventing ourselves from falling into temptations is extremely important. If you fall into temptation, it means you have not overcome it, grown weary, and shrunk back in your faith – none with which God is pleased.

When we keep ourselves alert and pray, the Holy Spirit teaches us to walk on the right path and we fight against and throw away our sins. Moreover, as much as our soul prospers, our heart will resemble that of our Lord, we will do well in every affair of life, and we will receive the blessing of good health.

Prayer is a key to having everything in our lives go well and receiving the blessing of good health in body and spirit. We have been promised in 1 John 5:18, *"We know that no one who is born of God sins; but He who was born of God keeps him, and the evil one does not touch him."* That's why when we keep ourselves alert, pray, and walk in the light, we will be kept safe from the enemy devil and even if we do fall into temptation, God will show us ways to escape it and, in all things, work for the good of those of you who love Him.

For God told us to pray continually, we must become His blessed children who lead our lives in Christ by keeping ourselves alert, driving away the enemy devil, and receiving everything with which God intends to bless us.

1 Thessalonians 5:23 tells us, *"Now may the God of peace Himself sanctify you entirely; and may your spirit and soul and body be preserved complete, without blame at the coming of our Lord Jesus Christ."*

May each of you receive the help of the Holy Spirit by keeping yourself alert and praying habitually, come to possess a blameless and spotless heart as a child of God by casting off all sinful natures within you and circumcising your heart by the Holy Spirit, enjoy the authority as His child in which your soul prospers, everything in your life is successful and you receive the blessing of good health, and give glory to God in everything you do, in the name of our Lord Jesus Christ I pray!

Chapter 5

Prayer of a Righteous Man

The effective prayer of a righteous man
can accomplish much.
Elijah was a man with a nature like ours,
and he prayed earnestly that it would not rain,
and it did not rain on the earth for three years and six months.
Then he prayed again,
and the sky poured rain and the earth produced its fruit.

James 5:16-18

1. Prayer of Faith that Heals the Sick

When we look back at our lives, there were times when we prayed in the midst of suffering and times when we praised and rejoiced after receiving God's answers. There were times when we prayed with others for the healing of our loved ones and times when we gave glory to God after accomplishing by prayer what had been impossible for man.

Found in Hebrews 11 are many references to faith. We are reminded in Verse 1 that *"Now faith is the assurance of things hoped for, the conviction of things not seen,"* while *"Without faith it is impossible to please Him, for he who comes to God must believe that He is and that He is a rewarder of those who seek Him"* (Verse 6).

Faith is largely separated into "fleshly faith" and "spiritual faith." On the one hand, by fleshly faith we can believe in God's Word only when the Word is in agreement with our thought. This fleshly faith does not bring any changes to our lives. On the other hand, by spiritual faith, we can believe in the power of the living God and His Word as it is even if it does not agree with our thought and theory. As we believe in the work of God who creates things out of nothingness, we experience tangible changes in our lives as well as His miraculous signs and wonders, and come to believe that everything is indeed possible for those who believe.

That is why Jesus told us, *"These signs will accompany those who have believed: in My name they will cast out demons, they will speak with new tongues; they will pick up serpents, and if they drink any deadly poison, it will not hurt them; they will lay hands on the sick, and they will recover"* (Mark 16:17-18), *"All things are possible to him who believes"* (Mark 9:23), and that *"Therefore I say to you, all things for which you pray and ask, believe that you have received them, and they will be granted you"* (Mark 11:24).

How can we possess spiritual faith and have firsthand experiences of our God's great power? Above all else, we must remember that the apostle Paul said in 2 Corinthians 10:5, *"We are destroying speculations and every lofty thing raised up against the knowledge of God, and we are taking every thought captive to the obedience of Christ."* We must no longer deem true the knowledge we have gathered to this point. Instead, we are to demolish every thought and theory which are in violation of God's Word, make ourselves obedient to His Word the truth, and live by it. As much as we demolish fleshly thoughts and cast off untruth within ourselves, our soul will prosper and we will possess spiritual faith by which we can believe.

Spiritual faith is the measure of faith God has given to each of us (Romans 12:3). After being preached the gospel and accepting Jesus Christ at first, our faith is as small as a mustard seed. As we continue to diligently attend worship services, hear

God's Word, and live by it, we become that much more righteous. Furthermore, as our faith grows into great faith, signs that accompany those who have believed will surely accompany us.

In praying to heal the sick, embedded in such prayer must be spiritual faith of those who pray. For the centurion – whose servant had become paralyzed and been in terrible suffering – featured in Matthew 8 had faith by which he believed his servant would be healed if Jesus only said the word, his servant was healed at that very hour (Matthew 8:5-13).

Moreover, when we pray for the sick, we must be bold in our faith and not doubt because, as God's Word tells us, *"But he must ask in faith without any doubting, for the one who doubts is like the surf of the sea, driven and tossed by the wind. For that man ought not to expect that he will receive anything from the Lord"* (James 1:6-7).

God is pleased with strong and steady faith that does not sway back and forth, and when we unite in love and pray for the sick with faith, God works even more greatly. For disease is the result of sin and God is the LORD our Healer (Exodus 15:26), when we confess our sins to one another and pray for each other, God gives us forgiveness and healing.

When you pray with spiritual faith and in spiritual love, you will experience God's great work, testify to our Lord's love, and honor Him.

2. Powerful and Effective is the Prayer of a Righteous Man

According to *The Merriam-Webster Dictionary,* a righteous man is someone who is "acting in accord with divine or moral law; free from guilt or sin." Yet, Romans 3:10 tells us that, *"There is none righteous, not even one."* And God says, *"It is not the hearers of the Law who are just before God, but the doers of the Law will be justified"* (Romans 2:13), and *"by the works of the Law no flesh will be justified in His sight; for through the Law comes the knowledge of sin"* (Romans 3:20).

Sin entered the world through the disobedience of Adam the first man created and countless people arrived at condemnation through the sin of one man (Romans 5:12, 18). To mankind who fell short of His glory, apart from the Law, the righteousness of God has been manifested, and even the righteousness of God comes through faith in Jesus Christ for all those who believe (Romans 3:21-23).

For this world's "righteousness" fluctuates according to each generation's values, it cannot be a true standard of righteousness. However, for God never changes, His righteousness can be the standard for true righteousness.

Therefore, it reads in Romans 3:28, *"we maintain that a man is justified by faith apart from works of the Law."* Yet, we do not nullify the law by our faith but rather establish it

(Romans 3:31).

If we become justified by faith, we must bear the fruit of arriving at holiness by being set free from sin and becoming slaves to God. We must strive to become truly righteous by casting off any untruths that are in violation of God's Word and living by His Word the truth itself.

God declares people "righteous" whose faith is accompanied by deed and who struggle to live by His Word day in and day out, and manifests His work in response to their prayer. How would God answer someone who attends church but has built a wall of sin between himself and God through disobedience to his parents, discord with his brothers, and committing of wrongdoings?

God makes the prayer of a righteous man – he who obeys and lives by God's Word and carries with him the proof of his love for God – powerful and effective by giving him the strength of prayer.

In Luke 18:1-18 is the Parable of the Persistent Widow. It features a widow and a case she brought before a judge who did not fear God and did not respect man. Even though the judge neither feared God nor cared much about men, he eventually ended up helping the widow. The judge said to himself, *"Even though I do not fear God nor respect man, yet because this widow bothers me, I will give her legal protection, otherwise by continually coming she will wear me out."* (vv. 4-5).

At the end of this parable Jesus said, *"Hear what the unrighteous judge said; now, will not God bring about justice for His elect who cry to Him day and night, and will He delay long over them? I tell you that He will bring about justice for them quickly"* (vv. 6-8).

When we look around, however, there are people who profess to be God's children, praying day and night and fasting frequently, yet do not receive His answers. Such individuals must come to realize that they have not yet become righteous in God's eyes.

Philippians 4:6-7 tells us, *"Be anxious for nothing, but in everything by prayer and supplication with thanksgiving let your requests be made known to God. And the peace of God, which surpasses all comprehension, will guard your hearts and your minds in Christ Jesus."* Depending on how much one has become "righteous" in God's sight and prays by faith and in love, the degree to which he receives God's answers will vary. After he has met the qualifications as a righteous man and prays, he can receive God's answers quickly and give glory to Him. Therefore, it is of utmost importance for people to tear down the wall of sin that stands in the way to God, come to possess qualifications to be declared "righteous" in God's eyes, and pray earnestly by faith and in love.

3. Gift and Power

"Gifts" are His presents that God gives freely and refer to a special work of God in His love. The more one prays, the more he will come to desire and ask for God's gift. At times, however, he may ask God for a gift in accordance with his deceitful desires. This is to bring on himself destruction and for this is *not right in God's eyes*, one must guard himself against it.

In Acts 8 is a sorcerer by the name of Simon who, after having been preached the gospel by Philip, followed Philip everywhere, and was astonished by the great signs and miracles he saw (Verses 9-13). When Simon saw that the Holy Spirit was given at the laying on of the hands of Peter and John, he offered the apostles money and asked them, *"Give this authority to me as well, so that everyone on whom I lay my hands may receive the Holy Spirit"* (Verses 17-19). In reply, Peter rebuked Simon: *"May your silver perish with you, because you thought you could obtain the gift of God with money! You have no part or portion in this matter, for your heart is not right before God. Therefore repent of this wickedness of yours, and pray the Lord that, if possible, the intention of your heart may be forgiven you. For I see that you are in the gall of bitterness and in the bondage of iniquity"* (Verses 20-23).

For gifts are given to those who show the living God and save mankind, they must be manifested under the Holy Spirit's supervision. Thus, before asking God for His gifts, we must first strive to become righteous in His eyes.

After our soul has prospered and we have molded ourselves into an instrument which God can use, He permits us to ask for gifts in the inspiration of the Holy Spirit and gives us the gifts for which we ask.

We know that each of our forefathers of faith was used by God for a range of purposes. Some greatly manifested God's power, others only prophesied without manifesting God's power, and still others only taught people. The more they possessed complete faith and love, God gave them greater power and allowed them to manifest greater work.

When he lived as a prince of Egypt, Moses' temper was so hot and quick that he killed in an instant an Egyptian who had ill-treated his fellow Israelites (Exodus 2:12). After many trials, however, Moses became a very humble man, more humble than anyone else on the face of the earth and then received great power. He brought the Israelites out of Egypt by manifesting a variety of signs and wonders (Numbers 12:3).

We also know the prayer of Prophet Elijah as written in James 5:17-18, *"Elijah was a man with a nature like ours, and he prayed earnestly that it would not rain, and it did not rain on the earth for three years and six months. Then he prayed again, and the sky poured rain and the earth produced its fruit."*

As we have seen and as the Bible tells us, the prayer of a righteous man is powerful and effective. Strength and power of a righteous man are distinguished. While there is a sort of prayer with which people are unable to receive God's answers even after countless hours of praying, there is also the prayer of great strength that brings down His answers as well as the manifestation of His power. God is delighted to accept prayer of faith, love, and sacrifice, and allows people to give glory to Him through various gifts and power He gives to people.

However, we were not righteous from the beginning; only after accepting Jesus Christ have we become righteous by faith. We become righteous as much as we become aware of sin by hearing His Word, cast off untruth, and have our soul prosper. Furthermore, for we will transform into more righteous men as much as we live and walk in the light and in righteousness, everyday of our lives must be changed by God so that we may also confess the way the apostle Paul did, *"I die every day"* (1 Corinthians 15:31).

I urge each of you to look back at your life leading up to this point and see whether a wall stands in your way to God and if so, tear it down without delay.

May each of you obey by faith, sacrifice in love, and pray as a righteous person so that you will be declared righteous, receive His blessings in everything you do, and give glory to God without reservation, in the name of our Lord I pray!

Chapter 6

If Two of You Agree on Earth

Again I say to you,
that if two of you agree on earth
about anything that they may ask,
it shall be done for them
by My Father who is in heaven.
For where two or three
have gathered together in My name,
I am there in their midst.

Matthew 18:19-20

1. God is Delighted to Accept Prayer in Agreement

A Korean proverb tells us, "It is better to lift together even a piece of paper." Instead of isolating oneself and trying to do everything on his own, this age-old adage teaches us, efficiency will rise and a better result can be expected when two or more people work together. Christianity that emphasizes on love for one's neighbors and church community must be a good example in this regard as well.

Ecclesiastes 4:9-12 tells us, *"Two are better than one because they have a good return for their labor. For if either of them falls, the one will lift up his companion. But woe to the one who falls when there is not another to lift him up. Furthermore, if two lie down together they keep warm, but how can one be warm alone? And if one can overpower him who is alone, two can resist him. A cord of three strands is not quickly torn apart."* These verses teach us that when people unite and collaborate, great power and joy can be produced.

By the same token, Matthew 18:19-20 tells us how important it is for believers to come together and pray in agreement. There are "individual prayer" through which people pray for their own problems on an individual basis or pray as they meditate on the Word in quiet times, and "prayer in agreement" through which a number of people gather to cry out to God.

As Jesus tells us "if two of you agree on earth" and "where two or three have gathered in My name," prayer in agreement refers to the prayer of many in one mind. God tells us that He is delighted to accept prayer in agreement and promises us He will do anything we ask Him and be present when two or three come together in the name of our Lord.

How can we give glory to God with answers we receive from Him through prayer in agreement at home and church, and within our group and cell? Let us delve into the significance and methods of prayer in agreement and make bread of its power so that we may receive from God anything as we pray for His kingdom, righteousness, and church, and greatly honor Him.

2. The Significance of Prayer in Agreement

In the first of the verses on which this Chapter is based, Jesus tells us, *"Again I say to you, that if two of you agree on earth about anything that they may ask, it shall be done for them by My Father who is in heaven"* (Matthew 18:19). Here we find something a little peculiar. Instead of referring to the prayer of "one person," "three people," or "two or more people," why did Jesus specifically say "if two of you agree on earth about anything they may ask for" and place the emphasis on "two" people?

"Two of you" here stands for, in relative terms, each of us "I" and the rest of the people. In other words, "two of you" can refer to one person, ten people, a hundred people, or a thousand people, in addition to oneself.

What, then, is the spiritual significance of the "two of you"? We have our own "self" and within us dwells the Holy Spirit with a character of His own. As Romans 8:26 reads, *"In the same way the Spirit also helps our weakness; for we do not know how to pray as we should, but the Spirit Himself intercedes for us with groanings too deep for words,"* the Holy Spirit who Himself intercedes for us makes our heart a temple in which to dwell.

We receive the authority to which we are entitled as children of God when we first believe Him and accept Jesus as our Savior. The Holy Spirit comes and revives our spirit who has been dead because of our original sin. Therefore, in each of God's children there are his own heart and the Holy Spirit with His own character.

"Two people on earth" means the prayer of our own heart and the prayer of our spirit which is the Holy Spirit's intercession (1 Corinthians 14:15; Romans 8:26). To say "two people on earth to agree about anything they ask for" means that these two prayers are offered up to God in agreement. Furthermore, when the Holy Spirit joins with one person in his prayer or two or more people in their prayer, it is for the "two of you" on earth to agree about anything you ask for.

By remembering the significance of prayer in agreement, we

must experience the fulfillment of the Lord's promise *"Again I say to you, that if two of you agree on earth about anything that they may ask, it shall be done for them by My Father who is in heaven"* (Matthew 18:19).

3. Methods of Prayer in Agreement

God is pleased to accept prayer in agreement, gives His answers quickly to such prayer, and manifests His great work because people pray to Him with one heart.

It will surely be a source of overflowing joy, peace, and infinite glory to God if the Holy Spirit and each of us pray with one heart. We would be able to bring down the "answer of fire" and unreservedly testify to the living God. Yet, becoming "one heart" is no easy task and bringing our heart to agreement carries a very significant implication.

Suppose a servant has two masters. Would not his loyalty and heart of service be naturally divided? The problem becomes more serious if the servant's two masters possessed different personalities and tastes.

Again, suppose two people came together to make plans for an event. Yet, if they failed to be of one mind and instead remained divided in their own opinions, it would be safer to conclude that things are not going too well. Moreover, if the two did their own work with two different goals in heart, their planning may appear to be going well on the outside but the outcome could not be more obvious. Therefore, the ability to be of one heart whether praying alone, with another person, or with two or more people is the key to receiving God's answer.

How, then, can we be of one heart in prayer?

People praying in agreement must pray in the inspiration of the Holy Spirit, be taken captive by the Holy Spirit, become one in the Holy Spirit, and pray in the Holy Spirit (Ephesians 6:18). For the Holy Spirit carries with Him the mind of God, He searches all things, even the depths of God (1 Corinthians 2:10) and intercedes for us according to the will of God (Romans 8:27). When we pray the way the Holy Spirit leads our mind, God is pleased to accept our prayer, gives us anything we ask, and even answers the desires of our heart.

In order to pray in the fullness of the Holy Spirit, we must believe in God's Word without doubting, obey in the truth, be joyful always, pray continually, and give thanks in all circumstances. We must also call out to God from our heart. When we show God faith that is accompanied by deed and wrestle in prayer, God is pleased and gives us joy through the Holy Spirit. This is said to be "filled with" and "being inspired by" the Holy Spirit.

Some new believers or those who have not been praying on a

regular basis have not yet received the power of prayer and thus tend to find prayer in agreement arduous and difficult. If such individuals attempt to pray for an hour, they try to come up with all kinds of prayer topics yet are unable to pray for the full hour. They grow weary and exhausted, anxiously wait for the time to pass quickly, and end up babbling in prayer. Such prayer is "the prayer of the soul" to which God cannot answer.

For many people, even if they have been attending church for more than a decade, their prayer is still the prayer of the soul. For most people who complain or become discouraged for the lack of God's answers cannot receive His answers because their prayer is that of the soul. Yet, this is not to say that God has turned His back on their prayer. God hears their prayer; He just cannot answer it.

Some may well ask, "Does this mean it is pointless to pray since we are praying without the inspiration of the Holy Spirit?" That is not the case, however. Even if they pray only in their thought, as they diligently call out to God the gates of prayer will open and they will receive the power of prayer and come to pray in spirit. Without prayer, the gates of prayer cannot be opened. For God listens even to the prayer of the soul, once the gates of prayer open, you will unite with the Holy Spirit, come to pray in the inspiration of the Holy Spirit, and receive answers for which you asked in the past.

Suppose there was a son who did not please his father. For

the son could not please his father by his deed, he could receive nothing he had asked from his father. Yet, one day the son began to please the father by deed and the father began to find his son after his own heart. Now, how would the father begin treating his son? Remember that their relationship was no longer what it used to be in the past. The father wished to give his son anything the latter asked him and the son received even the things he had asked for in the past.

By the same token, even if our prayer is from our thought, when it has piled up, we will receive the power of prayer and come to pray in a way that is pleasing to God as the gates of prayer open for you. We will also receive even the things for which we asked God in the past and realize that He has ignored not even one trivial item of our prayer.

Moreover, when we pray in spirit in the fullness of the Holy Spirit, we will not grow weary or succumb to sleepiness or worldly thoughts but pray by faith and in joy. This is how even a group of people can pray in agreement for they pray in spirit and in love with one mind and one will.

We read in the second of the verses on which this Chapter is based, *"For where two or three have gathered together in My name, I am there in their midst"* (Matthew 18:20). When people come together to pray in the name of Jesus Christ, God's children who have received the Holy Spirit are in essence praying in agreement, and our Lord will surely be where they are. In other words, when a group of people who have received the Holy Spirit gather and pray in agreement, our Lord will oversee the mind of each person, unite them by the Holy Spirit, and lead them to be of one mind so that their prayer will be pleasing to our God.

However, if a group of people cannot come together and be of one heart, the group as a whole cannot pray in agreement or pray from the heart of each participant even if they pray for a common goal because the heart of one participant is not in agreement with that of another in the group. If the heart of people in attendance cannot be united in one, the presider ought to lead a time of praise and repentance so that the heart of people gathered can become one in the Holy Spirit.

Our Lord will be with the praying people when they become one in the Holy Spirit, as He oversees and leads the heart of each individual in participation. When people's prayer is not in agreement, it must be understood that our Lord cannot be with such individuals.

When people become one in the Holy Spirit and pray in agreement, everyone will be praying from his heart, be filled with the Holy Spirit, sweat from their bodies, and become certain of God's answers for which they ask as a gust of joy from above enwraps them. Our Lord will be with people who pray in such a manner, and such prayer is the very kind that pleases God.

By praying in agreement in the fullness of the Holy Spirit and from your heart, I hope each of you will receive anything you ask for in prayer and thus give glory to God when you gather with others from your cell or group and at home or church.

The Great Power of Prayer in Agreement

One of the advantages of prayer in agreement is the difference in the speed at which people receive answers from God and the kind of work He manifests because, as an example, there is a drastic difference in quantity of prayer between a 30-minute prayer of one person with one request and a 30-minute prayer of ten people with the same request. When people pray in agreement and God is pleased to accept their prayer, they will experience the undeniable manifestation of God's work and the great power of their prayer.

In Acts 1:12-15, we find that after our Lord resurrected and ascended into heaven a group of people including His disciples joined together constantly in prayer. The number of people in that group was about a hundred and twenty. In earnest hope of receiving the Holy Spirit Jesus had promised them, these people gathered to pray in agreement until the day of Pentecost.

When the day of Pentecost had come, they were all together in one place. And suddenly there came from heaven a noise like a violent rushing wind, and it filled the whole house where they were sitting. And there appeared to them tongues as of fire distributing themselves, and they rested on each one of them. And they were all filled with the Holy Spirit and began to speak with other tongues, as the Spirit was giving them utterance (Acts 2:1-4).

How wondrous is this work of God? As they prayed in agreement, every one of the hundred and twenty people gathered received the Holy Spirit and began to speak in other tongues. The apostles also received great power from God so that the number of people who accepted Jesus Christ through Peter's message and were baptized stood at almost three thousand (Acts 2:41). As all kinds of wonders and miraculous signs were displayed by the apostles, the number of believers increased day after day and the life of believers began to change as well (Acts 2:43-47).

Now as they[the rulers and elders and scribes] observed the confidence of Peter and John and understood that they were uneducated and untrained men, they were amazed, and began to recognize them as having been with Jesus. And seeing the man who had been healed standing with them, they had nothing to say in reply (Acts 4:13-14).

At the hands of the apostles many signs and wonders were taking place among the people; and they were all with one accord in Solomon's portico. But none of the rest dared to associate with them; however, the people held them in high esteem. And all the more believers in the Lord, multitudes of men and women, were constantly added to their number, to such an extent that they even carried the sick out into the streets and laid them on cots and pallets, so that when Peter came by at least his shadow might fall on any one of them. Also the people from the cities in the vicinity of Jerusalem were coming together, bringing people who were sick or afflicted with unclean spirits, and they were all being healed (Acts 5:12-16).

It was the power of prayer in agreement that enabled the apostles to boldly preach the Word, heal the blind, the crippled, and the weak, revive the dead, heal all kinds of diseases, and drive out evil spirits.

The following is an account of Peter who was at the time imprisoned during the reign of Herod (Agrippa I) that was marked largely by his persecution on Christianity. In Acts 12:5 we find, *"So Peter was kept in the prison, but prayer for him was being made fervently by the church to God."* While Peter was asleep, bound with two chains, the church was praying in agreement for Peter. After God heard the church's prayer, He sent an angel to rescue Peter.

The night before Herod was to bring Peter to trial, the apostle was bound with two chains and asleep while sentries stood guard at the entrance (Acts 12:6). Yet, God manifested His power by unchaining the chains and having the iron gate of the prison open by itself (Acts 12:7-10). Upon his arrival at the house of Mary the mother of John, also called Mark, Peter found that many people had gathered and were praying for him (Acts 12:12). Such a miraculous work was the result of the power of the church's prayer in agreement.

All the church did for the imprisoned Peter was to pray in agreement. Likewise, when trouble engulfs a church or when sickness strikes believers, instead of employing man's thoughts and ways or worrying and becoming anxious, the children of God must first believe that He will solve all the problems in their hands and come together in one mind and pray in agreement.

God takes great interest in the church's prayer in agreement, is delighted in prayer in agreement, and answers such prayer with His miraculous works. Can you imagine how pleased God will be to see His children pray in agreement for His kingdom and righteousness?

As people become filled with the Holy Spirit and pray with their spirit when they come together to pray in agreement, they will experience God's great work. They will receive power to live by God's Word, bear witness to the living God the way early churches and apostles did, expand God's kingdom, and receive anything they ask.

Please keep in mind that our God has promised us He would answer us when we ask and pray in agreement. May each of you thoroughly understand the significance of the prayer in agreement and zealously meet with those who pray in the name of Jesus Christ, so that you will first have the experiences of the great power of prayer in agreement, receive the power of prayer, and become a precious worker testifying to the living God, in the name of our Lord I pray!

Chapter 7

You Ought to Pray
and Not to Lose Heart

Now He was telling them a parable to show that at all times they
ought to pray and not to lose heart, saying,

"In a certain city there was a judge
who did not fear God and did not respect man.
There was a widow in that city,
and she kept coming to him, saying,
'Give me legal protection from my opponent.'
For a while he was unwilling;
but afterward he said to himself,
'Even though I do not fear God nor respect man,
yet because this widow bothers me,
I will give her legal protection,
otherwise by continually coming she will wear me out.'"

And the Lord said, "Hear what the unrighteous judge said;
now, will not God bring about justice for His elect
who cry to Him day and night,
and will He delay long over them?
I tell you that He will bring about justice for them quickly."

Luke 18:1-8

1. The Parable of the Persistent Widow

When Jesus taught God's Word to the crowds, He did not speak to them without a parable (Mark 4:33-34). "The Parable of the Persistent Widow" on which this Chapter is based enlightens us on the importance of persistent prayer, how we are to pray always, and how we are not to give up.

How persistently do you pray to receive God's answers? Are you taking a break from praying or have you given up because God has yet to answer your prayer?

In life there are countless problems and issues both big and small. When we evangelize people and tell them of the living God, some seeking God begin attending church to solve their problems and others come to merely find comfort in their heart.

Regardless of the reasons for which people began attending church, as they worship God and accept Jesus Christ, they learn that they, as children of God, can receive anything they ask for and be transformed into men of prayer.

Thus, all children of God must learn through His Word the kind of prayer with which He is pleased, pray in accordance with the essentials to prayer, and possess faith to persevere and pray until they receive the fruit of God's answers. This is why people with faith are aware of the importance of prayer and pray habitually. They do not commit the sin of failing to pray even if they do not receive an answer right away. Instead of giving up, they pray even more fervently.

Only by such faith can people receive God's answers and give glory to Him. Yet, even though many people profess to believe, it is difficult to find people with such great faith as this. This is why our Lord laments and asks, *"However, when the Son of Man comes, will He find faith on the earth?"* (Luke 18:8).

In a certain town was an immoral judge to whom a widow kept coming and begged, "Give me legal protection from my opponent." This corrupt judge expected a bribe but the poor widow could not even afford a small token of appreciation to give the judge. Yet, the widow kept going to the judge and begged him and the judge kept refusing the widow's request. Then one day, he had a change of heart. Do you know why? Listen to what this immoral judge said to himself:

> *"Even though I do not fear God nor respect man, yet because this widow bothers me, I will give her legal protection, otherwise by continually coming she will wear me out!"* (Luke 18:4-5)

For the widow never gave up and kept going to him with her request, even this wicked judge could only succumb to the wishes of the widow who kept bothering him.

At the end of this parable which Jesus used to give us the key to receiving God's answers, He concluded, *"Hear what the unrighteous judge said; now, will not God bring about justice for His elect who cry to Him day and night, and will He delay long over them? I tell you that He will bring about justice for them quickly"* (vv. 6-8).

If an immoral judge listened to the plea of a widow, why would the righteous God not answer when His children call out to Him? If they vow to receive an answer for a specific problem, fast, stay up all night, and wrestle in prayer, how could God not answer them quickly? I am sure many of you have heard of instances in which people received His answers during a period of vowed prayer.

In Psalm 50:15 God tells us, *"Call upon Me in the day of trouble; I shall rescue you, and you will honor Me."* In other words, God intends for us to honor Him by answering our prayer. Jesus reminds us in Matthew 7:11, *"If you then, being evil, know how to give good gifts to your children, how much more will your Father who is in heaven give what is good to those who ask Him!"* How could God, who has without reservation given us His one and only Son to die for us, not answer the prayer of His beloved children? God desires to give quick answers to His children who love Him.

Yet, why do so many people say they are without His answers even though they pray? God's Word specifically tells us in Matthew 7:7-8, *"Ask, and it will be given to you; seek, and you will find; knock, and it will be opened to you. For everyone who asks receives, and he who seeks finds, and to him who knocks it will be opened.*" That's why it is impossible for our prayer to go unanswered. Yet, God is unable to answer our prayer because of a wall standing in our way to Him, because we have not prayed enough, or because the time has not yet arrived for us to receive His answers.

We are to pray always without giving up because when we persevere and keep praying by faith, the Holy Spirit tears down the wall that stands between God and us and opens the way to God's answers through repentance. When the amount of our prayer seems sufficient in God's eyes, He will surely answer us.

In Luke 11:5-8, Jesus teaches us again on perseverance and importunity:

> *Suppose one of you has a friend, and goes to him at midnight and says to him, "Friend, lend me three loaves; for a friend of mine has come to me from a journey, and I have nothing to set before him"; and from inside he answers and says, "Do not bother me; the door has already been shut and my children and I are in bed; I cannot get up and give you anything." I tell you, even though he will not get up and give him anything because he is his friend, yet because of his persistence he will get up and give him as much as he needs.*

Jesus teaches us that God does not refuse but answers His children's importunities. When we pray to God, we must pray boldly and with perseverance. It is not to say you just demand but pray and ask with a sense of certainty by faith. The Bible frequently mentions many forefathers of faith who received answers with such prayer.

After Jacob wrestled with an angel by the Jabbok River till daybreak, he earnestly prayed and made a strong demand for blessing, saying, *"I will not let you go unless you bless me"* (Genesis 32:26), and God permitted blessings for Jacob. From that point on, Jacob was called "Israel" and became the forefather of the Israelites.

In Matthew 15, a Canaanite woman whose daughter was suffering from demon-possession first came up to Jesus and called out to Him, *"Have mercy on me, Lord, Son of David; my daughter is cruelly demon-possessed."* But, Jesus did not say a word (Matthew 15:22-23). When the woman came the second time, knelt before Him, and begged Him, Jesus simply said, *"I was sent only to the lost sheep of the house of Israel,"* and refused the woman's request (Matthew 15:25-26). When the woman importuned Jesus once more, *"Yes, Lord; but even the dogs feed on the crumbs which fall from their masters' table,"* then Jesus said to her, *"O woman, your faith is great; it shall be done for you as you wish"* (Matthew 15:27-28).

Similarly, we have to follow the footsteps of our forefathers of faith in accordance with God's Word and always pray. And we ought to pray by faith, with a sense of certainty, and with a fervent heart. By faith in our God who allows us to reap at the proper time, we must become true followers of Christ in our prayer life without giving up.

2. Why We are to Pray Always

Just as man is unable to sustain life without breathing, the children of God who have received the Holy Spirit cannot arrive at eternal life without praying. Prayer is a dialogue with the living God and our spirit's breath. If God's children who have received the Holy Spirit do not communicate with Him, they will put out the Holy Spirit's fire and thus will no longer be able to walk on the path of life but rather go astray onto the path of death, and in the end fail to reach salvation.

Yet, for prayer establishes communication with God, we will arrive at salvation as we hear the voice of the Holy Spirit and learn and live by the will of God. Even if trouble comes our way, God will give us a way to avoid it. He will also work for our good in all things. By prayer we will also experience the power of the almighty God who strengthens us to confront and overcome the enemy devil, thereby giving glory to Him with our steadfast faith that can make what was impossible, possible.

Thus, the Bible commands us to pray without ceasing (1 Thessalonians 5:17) and this is "God's will" (1 Thessalonians 5:18). Jesus set for us a proper example of prayer by praying continually according to God's will irrespective of time and place. He prayed in the desert, on a mountain, and many other places, and prayed at dawn and nighttime.

By praying continually, our forefathers of faith lived by God's will. Prophet Samuel tells us, *"Moreover, as for me, far be it from me that I should sin against the LORD by ceasing to pray for you; but I will instruct you in the good and right way"* (1 Samuel 12:23). Prayer is God's will and His commandment; Samuel tells us that failing to pray constitutes a sin.

When we do not pray or take a break from our prayer life, worldly thoughts infiltrate our mind and prevent us from living by God's will and we come to face difficult problems for we are without God's protection. Thus, when people fall into temptation they grumble against God or go astray from His ways even more.

For this reason 1 Peter 5:8-9 reminds us, *"Be of sober spirit, be on the alert. Your adversary, the devil, prowls around like a roaring lion, seeking someone to devour. But resist him, firm in your faith, knowing that the same experiences of suffering are being accomplished by your brethren who are in the world"* and urge us to pray always. Let us pray not only when there are problems but always, so that we will be God's blessed children whose every affair in life goes well.

3. At the Proper Time We Will Reap a Harvest

Galatians 6:9 reads, *"Let us not lose heart in doing good, for in due time we will reap if we do not grow weary."* It is the same with prayer. When we pray always according to God's will without giving up and the proper time comes, we will reap a harvest.

If a farmer grows impatient soon after planting a seed and digs up the seed from the ground, or if he fails to care for the sprout and wait, what would be the point of trying to reap a harvest? Until we receive answers to our prayer, dedication and perseverance are necessary.

Moreover, the time of harvest varies according to the kind of the seeds planted. Some seeds bear fruit in a few months while others can take years. Vegetables and grain are harvested more easily than apples or such rare herbs as ginseng. For more precious and expensive crops, more time and dedication need to be invested.

You must realize that more prayer is required for bigger and more serious problems for which you pray. When Prophet Daniel saw a vision regarding the future of Israel, mourned for three weeks, and prayed, God heard Daniel's prayer the first day and sent an angel to make sure the prophet was aware of this (Daniel 10:12). However, as the prince of the power of the air resisted the angel for twenty-one days, the angel could come to

Daniel on the last day, and only then did Daniel come to know for sure (Daniel 10:13-14).

What would have happened if Daniel had given up and stopped praying? Even though he became distressed and lost strength after seeing the vision, Daniel pressed on in prayer and in the end received God's answer.

When we persevere by faith and pray until we receive His answers, God gives us a helper and leads us to His answers. That is why the angel who brought God's answers to Daniel told the prophet, *"But the prince of the kingdom of Persia was withstanding me for twenty-one days; then behold, Michael, one of the chief princes, came to help me, for I had been left there with the kings of Persia. Now I have come to give you an understanding of what will happen to your people in the latter days, for the vision pertains to the days yet future"* (Daniel 10:13-14).

For what kinds of problems do you pray? Is your prayer the kind that reaches God's throne? In order to understand the vision God had shown him, Daniel decided to humble himself as he did not eat any tasty food, nor did meat or wine enter his mouth, nor did he use any ointment at all until the entire three weeks were completed (Daniel 10:3). As Daniel humbled himself for those three weeks in vowed prayer, God heard his prayer and answered him on the first day.

Here, pay attention to the fact that while God heard Daniel's prayer and answered the prophet the first day, it took three weeks for His answers to reach Daniel. Many people, upon facing a serious problem, try praying for a day or two and are quick to give up. Such practice attests to their little faith.

What we need the most in our generation today is the heart with which we believe only in our God who surely answers us, persevere, and pray, regardless of the time of the arrival of God's answer. How can we expect to receive God's answers without perseverance?

God gives rain in its season, both the autumn rain and the spring rain, and sets the time of harvest (Jeremiah 5:24). That is why Jesus told us, *"Therefore I say to you, all things for which you pray and ask, believe that you have received them, and they will be granted you"* (Mark 11:24). For Daniel believed in God who answers prayer, he persevered and did not take a break from praying until he received God's answer.

The Bible tells us, *"Faith is the assurance of things hoped for, the conviction of things not seen"* (Hebrews 11:1). If anyone has given up praying because he has not yet received God's answer, he must not think he has faith or that he will receive God's answers. If he has true faith, he will not dwell in the present circumstances but instead pray continually without giving up. That's because he believes that God, who allows us to reap what we sow and repays us for what we have done, will surely answer him.

As Ephesians 5:7-8 reads, *"Therefore do not be partakers*

with them; for you were formerly darkness, but now you are Light in the Lord; walk as children of Light," may each of you possess true faith, persevere in prayer to the almighty God, and receive everything you ask for in prayer, and lead a life full of God's blessing, in the name of our Lord Jesus Christ I pray!

The Author:
Dr. Jaerock Lee

Dr. Jaerock Lee was born in Muan, Jeonnam Province, Republic of Korea, in 1943. In his twenties, Dr. Lee suffered from a variety of incurable diseases for seven years and awaited death with no hope for recovery. One day in the spring of 1974, however, he was led to a church by his sister and when he knelt down to pray, the Living God immediately healed him of all his diseases.

From the moment Dr. Lee met the Living God through that wonderful experience, he has loved God with all his heart and sincerity, and in 1978 he was called to be a servant of God. He prayed fervently so that he could clearly understand the will of God, wholly accomplish it and obey all the Words of God. In 1982, he founded Manmin Central Church in Seoul, Korea, and countless works of God, including miraculous healings and wonders, have been taking place at his church.

In 1986, Dr. Lee was ordained as a pastor at the Annual Assembly of Jesus' Sungkyul Church of Korea, and four years later in 1990, his sermons began to be broadcast in Australia, Russia, the Philippines, and many more through the Far East Broadcasting Company, the Asia Broadcast Station, and the Washington Christian Radio System.

Three years later in 1993, Manmin Central Church was selected as one of the "World's Top 50 Churches" by the *Christian World* magazine (US) and he received an Honorary Doctorate of Divinity from Christian Faith College, Florida, USA, and in 1996 a Ph. D. in Ministry from Kingsway Theological Seminary, Iowa, USA.

Since 1993, Dr. Lee has taken the lead in world mission through many overseas crusades in Tanzania, Argentina, L.A., Baltimore City, Hawaii, and New York City of the USA, Uganda, Japan, Pakistan, Kenya, the

Philippines, Honduras, India, Russia, Germany, Peru, Democratic Republic of the Congo, and Israel. In 2002 he was called a "worldwide pastor" by major Christian newspapers in Korea for his work in the various overseas Great United Crusades.

As of June of 2018, Manmin Central Church has a congregation of more than 130,000 members. There are 11,000 domestic and overseas branch churches throughout the globe, and so far more than 100 missionaries have been commissioned to 26 countries, including the United States, Russia, Germany, Canada, Japan, China, France, India, Kenya, and many more.

As of the date of this publishing, Dr. Lee has written 112 books, including bestsellers *Tasting Eternal Life before Death*, *My Life My Faith I & II*, *The Message of the Cross*, *The Measure of Faith*, *Heaven I & II*, *Hell*, and *The Power of God*. His works have been translated into more than 44 languages.

His Christian columns appear on *The Hankook Ilbo*, *The JoongAng Daily*, *The Dong-A Ilbo*, *The Munhwa Ilbo*, *The Seoul Shinmun*, *The Kyunghyang Shinmun*, *The Hankyoreh Shinmun*, *The Korea Economic Daily*, *The Shisa News*, and *The Christian Press*.

Dr. Lee is currently leader of many missionary organizations and associations: including Chairman, The United Holiness Church of Jesus Christ; President, Manmin World Mission; Permanent President, The World Christianity Revival Mission Association; Founder & Board Chairman, Global Christian Network (GCN); Founder & Board Chairman, World Christian Doctors Network (WCDN); and Founder & Board Chairman, Manmin International Seminary (MIS).

Heaven I & II

A detailed sketch of the gorgeous living environment the heavenly citizens enjoy and beautiful description of different levels of heavenly kingdoms.

The Message of the Cross

A powerful awakening message for all the people who are spiritually asleep! In this book you will find the reason Jesus is the only Savior and the true love of God.

Hell

An earnest message to all mankind from God, who wishes not even one soul to fall into the depths of hell! You will discover the never-before-revealed account of the cruel reality of the Lower Grave and hell.

Tasting Eternal Life Before Death

A testimonial memoirs of Dr. Jaerock Lee, who was born again and saved from the valley of death and has been leading an exemplary Christian life.

The Measure of Faith

What kind of a dwelling place, crown and reward are prepared for you in heaven? This book provides with wisdom and guidance for you to measure your faith and cultivate the best and most mature faith.

Awaken, Israel!

Why has God kept His eyes on Israel from the beginning of the world to this day? What kind of His providence has been prepared for Israel in the last days, who await the Messiah?

My Life My Faith I & II

Dr. Jaerock Lee's autobiography provides the most fragrant spiritual aroma for the readers, through his life extracted from the love of God blossomed in midst of the dark waves, cold yoke and the deepest despair.

The Power of God

A must-read that serves as an essential guide by which one can possess true faith and experience the wondrous power of God